Editor
Erica N. Russikoff, M.A.

Editor in Chief
Ina Massler Levin, M.A.

Creative Director
Karen J. Goldfluss, M.S. Ed.

Illustrator
Clint McKnight

Cover Artist
Barb Lorseyedi

Art Coordinator
Renée Mc Elwee

Imaging
Leonard P. Swierski

Publisher
Mary D. Smith, M.S. Ed.

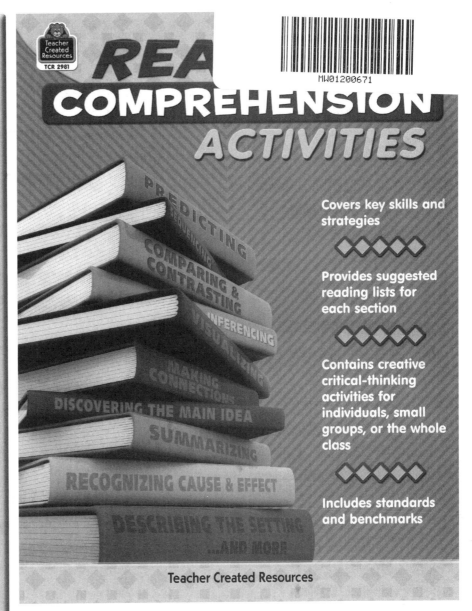

READING COMPREHENSION ACTIVITIES

TCR 2981

Covers key skills and strategies

Provides suggested reading lists for each section

Contains creative critical-thinking activities for individuals, small groups, or the whole class

Includes standards and benchmarks

PREDICTING · COMPARING & CONTRASTING · INFERENCING · VISUALIZING · MAKING CONNECTIONS · DISCOVERING THE MAIN IDEA · SUMMARIZING · RECOGNIZING CAUSE & EFFECT · DESCRIBING THE SETTING ...AND MORE

Teacher Created Resources

Authors

Jennifer Cripe, M.S. Ed.
Angela Vetter, M.S. Ed.

Teacher Created Resources
6421 Industry Way
Westminster, CA 92683
www.teachercreated.com

ISBN: 978-1-4206-2981-1

© *2011 Teacher Created Resources*
Made in U.S.A.

Table of Contents

Handwritten note at top right: O= Packet Project for a Novel

Introduction

Reading is an essential component throughout education. It enables students to be successful in all areas of the curricula. Comprehension is a skill that is necessary to create a love of reading, something that all teachers want for students. This book, *Reading Comprehension Activities*, provides teachers with engaging activities to teach the fundamental strategies and skills that build reading comprehension. This book focuses on the following specific reading strategies and skills:

Strategies	Skills	
• Predicting	• Summarizing	• Setting
• Context Clues	• Sequencing	• Problem and Solution
• Inferencing	• Retelling	• Cause and Effect
• Visualizing	• Main Idea	• Compare and Contrast
• Making Connections	• Characterization	

Reading Comprehension Activities contains a variety of activities for each of the different strategies and skills listed. Activities include teacher modeling, small group and center interactive work, and independent practice. These activities will enhance students' learning and can be used as a supplement to any core reading program. Many of the activities within this book allow teachers to use personal literature choices, giving the opportunity to provide differentiated instruction. A suggested book list is given at the beginning of each strategy or skill section. These books support the activities in each section.

Reading Comprehension Activities is designed to provide meaningful practice with the essential skills needed to succeed in reading. While students are actively engaged in these literacy activities, they will be challenged and will develop skills to apply to any independent reading selection.

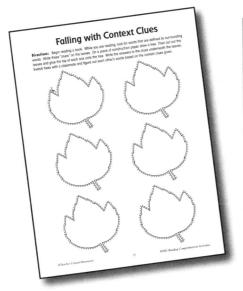

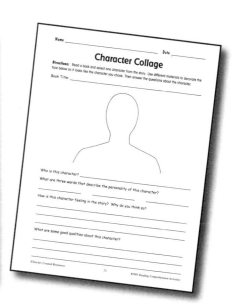

Standards and Benchmarks

Each activity in *Reading Comprehension Activities* meets at least one of the following standards and benchmarks, which are used with permission from McREL. Copyright 2011 McREL. Mid-continent Research for Education and Learning. 4601 DTC Boulevard, Suite 500, Denver, CO 80237. Telephone: 303-337-0990. Website: *www.mcrel.org/standards-benchmarks.* To align McREL Standards to the Common Core Standards, go to *www.mcrel.org.*

Standards and Benchmarks	Activity	Page(s)
Standard 5. Uses the general skills and strategies of the reading process		
Benchmark 1. Previews text (e.g., skims material, uses pictures, textual clues, and text format)	Chapter-by-Chapter Predictions	8
	Summarizing Predictions	9
	Processing Predictions	10
Benchmark 3. Makes, confirms, and revises simple predictions about what will be found in a text (e.g., uses prior knowledge and ideas presented in text, illustrations, titles, topic sentences, keywords, and foreshadowing clues)	Chapter-by-Chapter Predictions	8
	Summarizing Predictions	9
	Processing Predictions	10
Benchmark 5. Uses a variety of context clues to decode unknown words (e.g., draws on earlier reading, reads ahead)	Falling with Context Clues	13
	Context Clue Cards	14
	"What's the Context?" Cards	15–16
Benchmark 6. Uses word reference materials (e.g., glossary, dictionary, thesaurus) to determine the meaning, pronunciation, and derivations of unknown words	Falling with Context Clues	13
	Context Clue Cards	14
Standard 6. Uses skills and strategies to read a variety of literary texts		
Benchmark 1. Reads a variety of literary passages and texts (e.g., fairy tales, folktales, fiction, nonfiction, myths, poems, fables, fantasies, historical fiction, biographies, autobiographies, chapter books)	All activities	All activity pages
Benchmark 3. Understands the basic concept of plot (e.g., main problem, conflict, resolution, cause-and-effect)	What's the Problem?	80
	Problem and Solution Comic Strip	81–82
	Problem and Solution Storyboard	83
	What Caused the Effect?	86
	Cause and Effect Flap Booklet	89
Benchmark 4. Understands similarities and differences within and among literary works from various genres and cultures (e.g., in terms of settings, character types, events, point of view; role of natural phenomena)	Desert and Tundra Biomes	92–93
	Character Comparisons	94
	Alike and Different	95

Standards and Benchmarks *(cont.)*

Standards and Benchmarks	Activity	Page(s)
Standard 6. *(cont.)*		
Benchmark 5. Understands elements of character development in literary works (e.g., differences between main and minor characters; character's point of view; stereotypical characters as opposed to fully developed characters; changes that characters undergo; the importance of a character's actions, motives, and appearance to plot and theme)	Character Feelings Character Trait Cards Character Collage Character Comparisons	67 68–70 71 94
Benchmark 8. Makes connections between characters or simple events in a literary work and people or events in his or her own life	Connecting to Characters Making Connections Booklet Thoughtful Connections Bookmark	33 34–35 36
Standard 7. Uses skills and strategies to read a variety of informational texts		
Benchmark 5. Summarizes and paraphrases information in texts (e.g., includes the main idea and significant supporting details of a reading selection)	Soaring with Summaries Accordion Summaries Question Summaries Story Support Main Idea Flower Elephant Sort	39 40 41–43 61 62 63–64
Benchmark 6. Uses prior knowledge and experience to understand and respond to new information	All activities	All activity pages
Benchmark 7. Understands structural patterns or organization in informational texts (e.g., chronological, logical, or sequential order; compare-and-contrast; cause-and-effect; proposition and support)	A Crazy Weekend Game Board Sequencing Sequencing Caterpillar Retelling, from Start to Finish Chilly Retellings Chart a Story What Caused the Effect? Cause and Effect Matchup Cards Cause and Effect Flap Booklet Desert and Tundra Biomes Character Comparisons Alike and Different	46–47 48–49 50–51 54–55 56–57 58 86 87–88 89 92–93 94 95

Predicting

This strategy is crucial, as it makes students become more aware and attentive readers. In this section, teachers can help their students find clues in the text to make and revise predictions. Whether looking at chapter titles or finding proof in the text, students will become masters at making genuine predictions. The following reproducible pages can be used with any book, so students can practice predicting in different ways!

Suggested Books for Teaching Predicting

Bosch, Pseudonymous. *The Name of This Book Is Secret.* New York: Little, Brown, 2007.
　　Two unique 11-year-olds attempt to solve the mystery of a dead magician and prevent the evil Dr. L and Ms. Mauvais from finding the secret of immortality.

Catling, Patrick Skene. *The Chocolate Touch.* New York: HarperCollins, 1979.
　　John believes that chocolate is the best food in existence. But one day, after buying a special piece in a candy store, his perspective on chocolate changes.

Dahl, Roald. *Esio Trot.* New York: Viking, 1990.
　　Mr. Hoppy is out to win the heart of his true love by teaching her a spell that will make her tortoise grow larger.

———. *Fantastic Mr. Fox.* New York: Alfred A. Knopf, 1970.
　　Three bad-tempered farmers do everything they can in order to get rid of Mr. Fox and his family.

DiCamillo, Kate. *The Magician's Elephant.* Somerville, MA: Candlewick, 2009.
　　Peter, an orphan, has questions when a fortune-teller's tent mysteriously appears in the market square. Little does he know, the fortune-teller's answer (an elephant!) begins a chain of surprising events.

Activities for Predicting

Chapter-by-Chapter Predictions

Copy Chapter-by-Chapter Predictions (page 8) for each student. Have students begin reading a chapter book. In each square on page 8, students will predict what will happen in each chapter. They will continue through each chapter of their text. For fun, allow students time to share their predictions.

Summarizing Predictions

Copy Summarizing Predictions (page 9) for each student. Have students begin reading a chapter book. As they read, they will summarize the story, make predictions, and analyze their predictions in the appropriate boxes. They should also identify the chapters and page numbers so they can reference the story details. After students have read beyond their first predictions, have them complete this activity a second time.

Processing Predictions

Copy Processing Predictions (page 10) for each student. Have students begin reading a book. Then have them write a summary of what they have read so far. Next, have students make predictions and use details from the text to support the predictions. Have students continue reading the story and then write another summary of what has happened. Then have them analyze their predictions.

Chapter-by-Chapter Predictions

Directions: Begin reading a chapter book. Make predictions for each chapter in the boxes below.

Book Title: _____

Chapter _____	Chapter _____

Chapter _____	Chapter _____

Chapter _____	Chapter _____

Name _____ Date _____

Summarizing Predictions

Directions: Begin reading a chapter book. Provide a summary for what you have read. Then write a prediction for what you think will happen next. Include details from the text that support your prediction. Analyze your prediction, circling the appropriate answer. Continue reading, and then complete these steps a second time.

Book Title: _____

Chapter or Pages: _____   Chapter or Pages: _____

Summary	Summary
_____ _____ _____ _____ _____ _____	_____ _____ _____ _____ _____ _____
Prediction	**Prediction**
_____ _____ _____ _____ _____ _____	_____ _____ _____ _____ _____ _____
Details from book that support prediction _____ _____ _____ _____ My prediction was correct/incorrect. *(Circle one.)*	Details from book that support prediction _____ _____ _____ _____ My prediction was correct/incorrect. *(Circle one.)*

Processing Predictions

Directions: Begin reading a book. Provide a summary for what you have read. Then write a prediction for what you think will happen next. Include details from the text that support your prediction. Continue reading the story. Write another summary, and then analyze your prediction.

Book Title: _____

Read pages _____

What has happened in the story so far? _____

_____

_____

_____

What do you think will happen next? _____

_____

_____

What are some details from the story that support your prediction?

_____

_____

Continue reading the story until page _____

What happened in the story? _____

_____

_____

_____

Was your prediction correct or incorrect? Why? _____

_____

_____

Context Clues

In this section, teachers will find creative context clue activities for students to practice this necessary strategy. By being alert to context clues, students can find the meanings of unfamiliar words, increasing their vocabulary and overall reading comprehension. The following pages include two reproducibles that can be used with any book and a vocabulary matching activity. These activities will help students practice using surrounding words in order to understand tricky text.

Suggested Books for Teaching Context Clues

Blume, Judy. *Blubber.* Scarsdale, NY: Bradbury Press, 1974.
    Because her fifth-grade class is tormenting a classmate, Jill follows suit. But eventually, Jill discovers how it feels to also be the target.

Bryant, Jen. *A River of Words: The Story of William Carlos Williams.* Grand Rapids, MI: Eerdmans Books, 2008.
    In this picture book, William Carlos Williams' life is depicted, from childhood to adulthood.

Frost, Helen. *Diamond Willow.* New York: Farrar, Straus and Giroux, 2008.
    A 12-year-old Alaskan girl, Willow, wants to take her wounded dog to her grandparents' house. Trouble arises mid-journey when they get caught in a blizzard.

Lin, Grace. *Where the Mountain Meets the Moon.* New York: Little, Brown, 2009.
    Minli lives in a meager hut with her parents. At night, her father tells wondrous folktales that stir Minli's imagination—so much so that she sets off on a journey to change her family's fortune.

Paulsen, Gary. *Mudshark.* New York: Wendy Lamb Books, 2009.
    Principal Wagner can deal with many problems, but when 65 erasers go missing, he asks 12-year-old Lyle Williams, or "Mudshark," for help.

Activities for Context Clues

Falling with Context Clues

Copy Falling with Context Clues (page 13) for each student. Also, give each student his or her own piece of 12" x 18" construction paper. Have them draw a tree on the paper. Have students begin reading a book and, while they are reading, have them locate words that can be defined using context clues. On the leaves, students will write the context clues that help define the words. Students will then cut out the leaves and glue the top portion of them onto the trees, making sure the majority of each leaf can still be lifted up. Once all the leaves are glued, students will write the answers to the word puzzles they created underneath the leaves. Have students switch trees with classmates and figure out each other's context clue puzzles. For fun, hang up the trees for a wonderful fall display.

Context Clue Cards

Copy Context Clue Cards (page 14) for each student. Have students begin reading a chapter book. As they read their text, they should be alert to difficult or unknown words. They will write these words on the context clue cards. Next, they will write the clues that the text provides for the word meanings. After this step, students will make a guess as to what each word means and then look up the word to discover its true meaning. Students will continue to do this throughout the text in order to learn a variety of new vocabulary words.

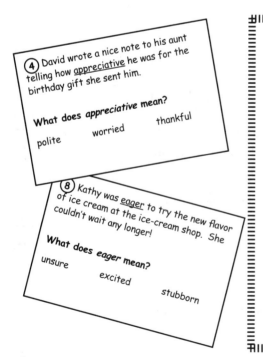

4 David wrote a nice note to his aunt telling how <u>appreciative</u> he was for the birthday gift she sent him.

What does appreciative mean?

polite   worried   thankful

8 Kathy was <u>eager</u> to try the new flavor of ice cream at the ice-cream shop. She couldn't wait any longer!

What does eager mean?

unsure   excited   stubborn

"What's the Context?" Cards

These context clue cards are an engaging way for students to practice this essential reading strategy. To begin, copy "What's the Context?" Cards (page 15) onto cardstock and laminate for durability. Cut out the cards. Then copy "What's the Context?" Cards Recording Sheet (page 16) for each student. Students will use context clues to find the meaning of the underlined word in each sentence. Once they figure out the meaning, they will write both the underlined word and the word meaning on the recording sheet. Additionally, students will read the passage at the bottom of the recording sheet and determine the meaning of the underlined words. Then they will circle the appropriate choices.

Falling with Context Clues

Directions: Begin reading a book. While you are reading, look for words that are defined by surrounding words. Write these "clues" on the leaves. On a piece of construction paper, draw a tree. Then cut out the leaves and glue the top of each one onto the tree. Write the answers to the clues underneath the leaves. Switch trees with a classmate and figure out each other's words based on the context clues given.

Context Clue Cards

Directions: Begin reading a chapter book. When you come across a difficult or unknown word, write it in a box. Then write down clues that help you to understand the meaning of the word. Make a guess as to what the word means and write it on the line. Then find the definition in the dictionary and write it on the line, as well.

Book Title: _____

Word: _____ Clue: _____ _____ Guess: _____ _____ Definition: _____ _____	Word: _____ Clue: _____ _____ Guess: _____ _____ Definition: _____ _____
Word: _____ Clue: _____ _____ Guess: _____ _____ Definition: _____ _____	Word: _____ Clue: _____ _____ Guess: _____ _____ Definition: _____ _____
Word: _____ Clue: _____ _____ Guess: _____ _____ Definition: _____ _____	Word: _____ Clue: _____ _____ Guess: _____ _____ Definition: _____ _____
Word: _____ Clue: _____ _____ Guess: _____ _____ Definition: _____ _____	Word: _____ Clue: _____ _____ Guess: _____ _____ Definition: _____ _____

"What's the Context?" Cards

1 James could not believe the <u>rancid</u> smell coming from the refrigerator. He discovered it was from the rotten broccoli.

What does *rancid* mean?

fresh   disgusting   spicy

2 Shane was <u>lethargic</u> the next morning after staying up past his bedtime reading his favorite books.

What does *lethargic* mean?

tired   ready   thirsty

3 Elizabeth had a <u>solemn</u> look on her face after losing the championship softball game.

What does *solemn* mean?

helpful   anxious   sad

4 David wrote a nice note to his aunt telling how <u>appreciative</u> he was for the birthday gift she sent him.

What does *appreciative* mean?

polite   worried   thankful

5 Henry was <u>petrified</u> after seeing strange shadows on his bedroom walls while he was trying to fall asleep.

What does *petrified* mean?

scared   happy   grumpy

6 Ginger looked <u>attractive</u> in her ruffled pink dress, sparkly shoes, and new haircut.

What does *attractive* mean?

energized   pretty   little

7 Peyton was helping his family <u>conserve</u> water by taking shorter showers in the mornings.

What does *conserve* mean?

waste   save   heat

8 Kathy was <u>eager</u> to try the new flavor of ice cream at the ice-cream shop. She couldn't wait any longer!

What does *eager* mean?

unsure   excited   stubborn

"What's the Context?" Cards
Recording Sheet

Directions: Read each numbered card. Use context clues to figure out the meaning of the underlined words. Write the underlined words, as well as their matching word meanings, on the lines below.

Underlined Word	Word Meaning
1. _____	_____
2. _____	_____
3. _____	_____
4. _____	_____
5. _____	_____
6. _____	_____
7. _____	_____
8. _____	_____

Directions: Read the passage below. Circle the words that match the meaning of the underlined words.

Shawn was walking into the grocery store with his mom when he saw an older lady walking slowly toward the door. Shawn wanted to be <u>courteous</u>, so he held the door open for the lady. The lady thanked him for being such a gentleman. Shawn became <u>bashful</u>, his cheeks turning red. He then quietly walked into the store.

1. **What does *courteous* mean?**

   rushed   funny   polite

2. **What does *bashful* mean?**

   sad   shy   healthy

Inferencing

Making inferences can be a very difficult but rewarding strategy for children to master. This section provides activities that will help students form conclusions based on textual clues. The included matching activity can be done in a small-group or a whole-class setting. Another activity allows students to read and draw conclusions about an unknown text. An additional reproducible can be used with any text in order to help students practice inferencing.

Suggested Books for Teaching Inferencing

Babbitt, Natalie. *Tuck Everlasting.* New York: Farrar, Straus and Giroux, 1975.
    The Tuck family has an unusual secret. Thanks to a special spring, they have looked the same for 87 years! When a young girl discovers their secret, the Tuck family educates her on life and death. A malicious stranger overhears and plans to take control of the spring. The Tuck family stops him.

Cleary, Beverly. *Strider.* New York: HarperCollins, 1991.
    Leigh, a 14-year-old boy, is processing his parents' divorce, his new attachment to an abandoned dog, his personal insecurities, and his thoughts about a girl.

Gardiner, John Reynolds. *Stone Fox.* New York: HarperCollins, 1980.
    Willy is training hard in order to win a dog-sled race. He wants to win the money from the race and give it to his grandfather, who is about to lose his farm.

Salisbury, Graham. *Calvin Coconut: Trouble Magnet.* New York: Wendy Lamb Books, 2009.
    Calvin, a fourth-grader, isn't great at taking care of his responsibilities. He'd rather have fun with his friends than face a bully, the new teacher, or his new houseguest.

Stead, Rebecca. *When You Reach Me.* New York: Wendy Lamb Books, 2009.
    Miranda and her best friend, Sal, are familiar with their New York City neighborhood. Nothing is out of the ordinary—that is, until the mysterious, sometimes future-predicting notes arrive.

Activities for Inferencing

Making Inferences One Step at a Time

Copy Making Inferences One Step at a Time (page 19), one per student. Have students begin reading a book. Have students write down phrases or sentences from the story that help them figure out what is happening. Then have them write down what they already know about these ideas. Finally, have them write down what they can infer about the story using this information. Students can continue reading and then complete these steps a second time.

Who, What, and *Where* Inferences

Copy *Who*, *What*, and *Where* Inferences (page 20) for each student. Have students read the passage and work through the questions, finding hints to support each answer.

"What Is Kevin Doing?" Cards

This activity allows students to practice making inferences using small passages. Copy "What Is Kevin Doing?" Cards (pages 21–22) onto cardstock and laminate for durability. Cut out the cards. Then copy "What Is Kevin Doing?" Cards Recording Sheet (page 23) for each student. Have students read the cards and match each one to the event it describes. After students have matched each card, they will record each answer next to the appropriate number. Then they will write down the words that helped them figure out each answer. Additionally, students will read the passage at the bottom of the recording sheet and determine what Kevin is doing.

Making Inferences One Step at a Time

Directions: Begin reading a book. In the boxes below, write down phrases or sentences from the story that help you figure out what is happening. Then write down what you already know about these ideas. Finally, write down what you can infer about the story using this information. Continue reading and then complete these steps a second time.

Book Title: _____

What the Author Writes	What I Already Know	What I Can Infer
Page: ____		
Page: ____		

Who, *What*, and *Where* Inferences

Directions: Read the passage. Answer the questions and find hints to support each answer.

It was finally Friday! My family and I were so excited! After spending all week packing our suitcases, we were ready to go to the airport. Luckily, our plane was on time. After landing and getting to the hotel, we were ready to go sightseeing.

The first stop was breathtaking. Listening to the sound of the water was like hearing thunder over and over. You could feel the cool mist on your face, which made me want to put on my sweatshirt. Looking over the edge  was scary at times; it sent a chill down my spine as the fear of falling set in. The white wall of water that cascaded down the side was amazing to see. After enjoying the view for a while, everyone got together at the observation deck. We all crammed in, my brother kneeling on the ground next to my sister, and said, "Cheese!" It was a wonderful day of sightseeing, and I can't wait to see what the family gets to do tomorrow.

1. Who is the passage about? _____

_____

Hints: _____

_____

2. What is happening in the passage? _____

_____

Hints: _____

_____

3. Where is the author of the passage? _____

_____

Hints: _____

_____

4. What could happen next in the passage? _____

_____

Hints: _____

_____

"What Is Kevin Doing?" Cards

(1) Kevin enters the kitchen. He can smell the disgusting aroma filling the room. He knows he had better get rid of the stench. He tosses the bag over his shoulder and heads outside.

What is Kevin doing?

doing his homework

(2) Kevin grabs his folder. He takes out a pencil and sharpens it. He walks over to his desk, which is piled high with heavy books. After looking through his folder, he finds what he needs. He begins to write.

What is Kevin doing?

wrapping a present

(3) Kevin squirts some soap into the sink while it is filling up with water. Bubbles start to rise. He looks through the drawers nearby for a sponge and some gloves.

What is Kevin doing?

taking out the trash

(4) Kevin places the shirt into a small box. He finds a roll of paper covered in balloons and streamers. Kevin cuts a large piece of paper and covers the box. Now it is ready!

What is Kevin doing?

washing some dishes

"What Is Kevin Doing?" Cards *(cont.)*

⑤ Kevin grabs his water bottle and puts it into his backpack. He looks at the steep mountain ahead. He is excited to be out in nature! **What is Kevin doing?**	watching a movie
⑥ Kevin watches the quarterback huddle with his team. Kevin looks at the score. His favorite team is winning! **What is Kevin doing?**	fishing
⑦ Kevin takes out some money to pay the lady for the ticket. He walks to the concession stand to buy some popcorn and a soda. After getting his snacks, he finds his perfect seat, just as the lights dim. **What is Kevin doing?**	taking a hike
⑧ Kevin grabs his hat and his tackle box and heads down to the river. He sits down on the edge and places some bait on his grandpa's old pole. Kevin watches the calmness of the river and waits patiently. **What is Kevin doing?**	watching a football game

Name _____   Date _____

"What Is Kevin Doing?" Cards
Recording Sheet

Directions: Read each card, and then match the card to the event it describes. Write the answer next to the correct number below. Next to the answer, write down the words that helped you figure out the answer.

	Passage Answer	**Word Hints from Passage**
1.	_____	_____
2.	_____	_____
3.	_____	_____
4.	_____	_____
5.	_____	_____
6.	_____	_____
7.	_____	_____
8.	_____	_____

Directions: Read the passage below and underline the clues that help you figure out what Kevin is doing. Then write your answer below.

Kevin puts on his heavy jacket, wool hat, and gloves. He grabs his newly waxed board and heads out the door toward the lifts. Snow flurries are gently falling, and the air is cold. Kevin hops onto the lift and rides all the way to the top of the mountain, which is covered in white powder. As he nears the top, he slides his foot onto his board and begins his exciting adventure down the mountain.

What is Kevin doing? _____

Visualizing

Visualizing can make reading come alive for young readers. In this strategy section, students will be able to use their imaginations to help create "mind pictures" of what happens in the stories they read. Teachers can instruct students how to use their senses to fully experience any text, known or unknown. For two activities, students will read and visualize an unknown text. For the third activity, students will read and describe any given text.

Suggested Books for Teaching Visualizing

Anderson, Laurie Halse. *Fever 1793.* New York: Simon & Schuster, 2000.
    After a wave of yellow fever strikes Philadelphia, 16-year-old Matilda must leave the city with her grandfather. After some time, they return, with Matilda having changed into a much stronger and more mature young woman.

Bridges, Ruby. *Through My Eyes.* New York: Scholastic, 1999.
    Ruby describes, as a six-year-old, what it was like to live in 1960 when her school in New Orleans was being integrated.

Byrd, Robert. *Leonardo: Beautiful Dreamer.* New York: Dutton, 2003.
    Through text and vivid illustrations, Leonardo da Vinci's life—as both a scientist and an artist—and work are depicted.

Juster, Norton. *The Phantom Tollbooth.* New York: Random House, 1961.
    Milo thinks that everything is a waste of time. However, when a mysterious tollbooth shows up in his bedroom, his curiosity gets the better of him, and he can't resist but to pay the toll and drive his toy car past the entry. What happens next is anything but boring!

O'Brien, Robert C. *Mrs. Frisby and the Rats of Nimh.* New York: Atheneum, 1971.
    A widowed mouse with a sick child must turn to some unusually gifted rats for help.

Activities for Visualizing

What Do You See?

Copy What Do You See? (page 26), one per student. Have students copy one or two sentences that they visualized from the book. Then have them analyze and create images for what they imagined.

Imaginative Mind Pictures

Copy the first page of Imaginative Mind Pictures (page 27) multiple times onto cardstock and laminate for durability. Cut out the passages. Then copy the second page of Imaginative Mind Pictures (page 28) for each student. For this activity, students will select one of the passages and read it carefully. As they read, students will imagine what is happening and draw detailed pictures of what is going on in the text. Afterwards, students will write a few sentences describing the pictures they drew. This activity will really get imaginations working!

Use Your Imagination

This activity will give students the opportunity to be the author and write a passage to visualize. Copy "Use Your Imagination" Cards (page 29) onto cardstock and laminate for durability. Cut out the cards. Then copy Use Your Imagination (page 30) for each student. For this activity, students will select one of the cards to read. As they read, students will use their senses to imagine what is happening and then draw detailed pictures depicting what they imagine. Then students will write paragraphs describing their pictures.

Name _____ Date _____

What Do You See?

Directions: Read a book, and then choose a part from the story that you could visualize and write about it below. Draw a picture of what you imagined as you read.

Book Title: _____

Page: _____

Copy one or two sentences that you visualized from the book.

_____

_____

_____

_____

Describe what you imagined as you read this part.

_____

_____

_____

_____

Draw a picture of what you imagined.

Imaginative Mind Pictures

Passage #1

In the middle of the blue lake surrounded by tall pine trees, I sat with my grandpa in his old boat. We each had a fishing pole in our hands, hoping to feel something tug from under the calm water below. My grandpa quietly sat back in his weathered overalls and straw hat, smiling at me every once in a while. The sun's bright light lit up the sky. To keep the sun from my eyes, I wore my favorite green baseball cap. After a while, I looked down into the water to see a few fish swimming nearby. I was excited at the chance of catching one of them.

Passage #2

We finally made it to the beach! My family and I unpacked the car, walked across the sand, and found the perfect spot to sit. My brother and I laid out the towels and set up the colorful striped umbrella. My mom and dad arranged the ice coolers, which were filled with sandwiches and water bottles. As we settled down in our spot, I looked out to see the ocean's blue water and the many surfers out on the waves. I also saw a few little kids building sand castles nearby. My mom rested on her towel and began reading a book. My brother put on some sunscreen and his favorite orange sun hat. My dad and I stood up—we were ready to get into the water and swim!

Name _____ Date _____

Imaginative Mind Pictures *(cont.)*

Directions: Read a passage to yourself and try to imagine what is happening. Write down the passage number and draw a picture of what you see in your mind. Afterwards, write a few sentences describing your picture.

Passage # _____

_____

_____

_____

_____

_____

_____

_____

_____

"Use Your Imagination" Cards

You just won tickets to your favorite concert.	You're going to watch cars race today.
The carnival is tonight, and you can't wait to go.	Your alarm went off an hour ago, and now you're late for school.
You're having fun at the zoo.	It's time for the family summer vacation.
You can't wait to go camping.	You're going to help make dinner tonight.
It's your birthday!	You've found a lost pet.

Use Your Imagination

Directions: Read a card to yourself and use your senses to imagine what is happening. Draw a picture of what you see in your mind. Then write a paragraph describing your picture.

Making Connections

This strategy is essential to the success of any reader. With different types of graphic organizers, teachers can effectively help their students relate to texts on many levels. Students can practice making connections using the included exploratory and thought-provoking activities.

Suggested Books for Teaching Making Connections

Barshaw, Ruth McNally. *Ellie McDoodle: New Kid in School.* New York: Bloomsbury, 2008.
Ellie feels like an outcast at her new school. She's an avid reader with a name teachers often stumble over. But when her classmates need help rallying against an important cause (unfair lunch lines!), she offers up her services.

Blume, Judy. *Superfudge.* New York: Dutton, 1980.
Twelve-year-old Peter already has one troublesome brother, Fudge, to contend with. When he finds out his parents are having another baby, Peter wonders if the child will be anything like Fudge.

Henkes, Kevin. *Sun & Spoon.* New York: Greenwillow Books, 1997.
Spoon is having difficulty grieving over his grandmother's death, so he steals a personal memento of hers. Little does he know, it is the same memento his grandfather was clutching onto to preserve her memory.

Kinney, Jeff. *Diary of a Wimpy Kid.* New York: Amulet Books, 2007.
Through diary entries and hand-drawn cartoons, Greg documents his middle-school experiences as he and his best friend, Rowley, "survive" girls, bullies, and the struggles of friendship.

Park, Barbara. *Skinnybones.* New York: Knopf Books, 1982.
Alex, otherwise known as "Skinnybones," is the smallest kid on the baseball team. Still, he unwisely brags to the best baseball player, T. J. Stoner, resulting in a pitching contest.

Activities for Making Connections

Connecting to Characters

With this activity, your students will be able to practice making connections with characters from their stories. Copy Connecting to Characters (page 33) for each student. After reading any selected text, students will complete the questions on the page and draw a picture of the character to which they can relate. This can lead to a great book discussion!

Making Connections Booklet

Copy Making Connections Booklet (pages 34–35) for each student. Give each student a piece of 8 1/2" x 11" construction paper. Have students read a book and then answer the questions about setting, characters, problems, and favorite parts. Then have them cut out the boxes, staple them together, and add a cover using the construction paper in order to create their booklets. This making-connections activity can be used a variety of times throughout the year.

Thoughtful Connections Bookmark

This bookmark can be used with any text and is a great way for students to practice making connections. Copy Thoughtful Connections Bookmark (page 36) for each student. Have students fold their pages in half. Then have students begin reading a book. As they read, they will make connections on both sides of the bookmark. First, they will document what they read. Next, they will explain what this made them think of. Then they will analyze the connection.

Name _____ Date _____

Connecting to Characters

Directions: Read a book, and then draw a picture of a character from your story that you can relate to in some way. Answer the questions about your character below.

Book Title: _____

What is the character's name?

_____

How is this character like you?

_____

_____

What personality traits do you have in common?

_____

_____

Give an example from the story that shows the character's personality.

_____

_____

What feelings does this character have that you can relate to?

_____

_____

What is the main problem this character faces?

_____

_____

If you were this character, how would you solve the problem?

_____

_____

Making Connections Booklet

Directions: Read a book, and then answer the questions about the setting and characters. Cut out the boxes and staple them to the boxes on page 35. Using construction paper, add a cover with your name, the book title, and the author. Now you have a Making Connections Booklet!

What does the setting look like? Does it remind you of a place you have been? Explain.

_____

_____

_____

_____

Draw a picture of the setting below.

Tell about someone in your life that reminds you of a character in the book. Explain how they are the same and how they are different.

_____

_____

_____

_____

Draw a picture of this person and the character below.

Making Connections Booklet *(cont.)*

Directions: Answer the questions about problems and favorite parts. Cut out the boxes and staple them to the boxes on page 34. Using construction paper, add a cover with your name, the book title, and the author. Now you have a Making Connections Booklet!

What is the problem in the story? What do the characters do to solve it?

_____

_____

_____

_____

Draw a picture of the problem below.

What is your favorite part of the story? Why is it your favorite part?

_____

_____

_____

_____

Draw a picture of your favorite part below.

Name _____   Date _____

Thoughtful Connections Bookmark

Directions: Begin reading a book. Write down your thoughts about the story, and make two connections below. Write the appropriate connection type (text-to-text, text-to-self, or text-to-world) on the line.

text-to-text = relates to something else you've read

text-to-self = relates to yourself

text-to-world = relates to something that happened in the world

Book Title: _____

_____

I read about . . .

_____

_____

_____

_____

_____

_____

This made me think of . . .

_____

_____

_____

_____

_____

_____

I made a text-to-_____ connection.

---

text-to-text = relates to something else you've read

text-to-self = relates to yourself

text-to-world = relates to something that happened in the world

Book Title: _____

_____

I read about . . .

_____

_____

_____

_____

_____

_____

This made me think of . . .

_____

_____

_____

_____

_____

_____

I made a text-to-_____ connection.

Summarizing

Being able to concisely summarize what one has read is a critical skill every reader needs to master. In this section, teachers will be able to strengthen their students' abilities to summarize text. Each of the following reproducibles will help students discover and write about the main ideas of a story.

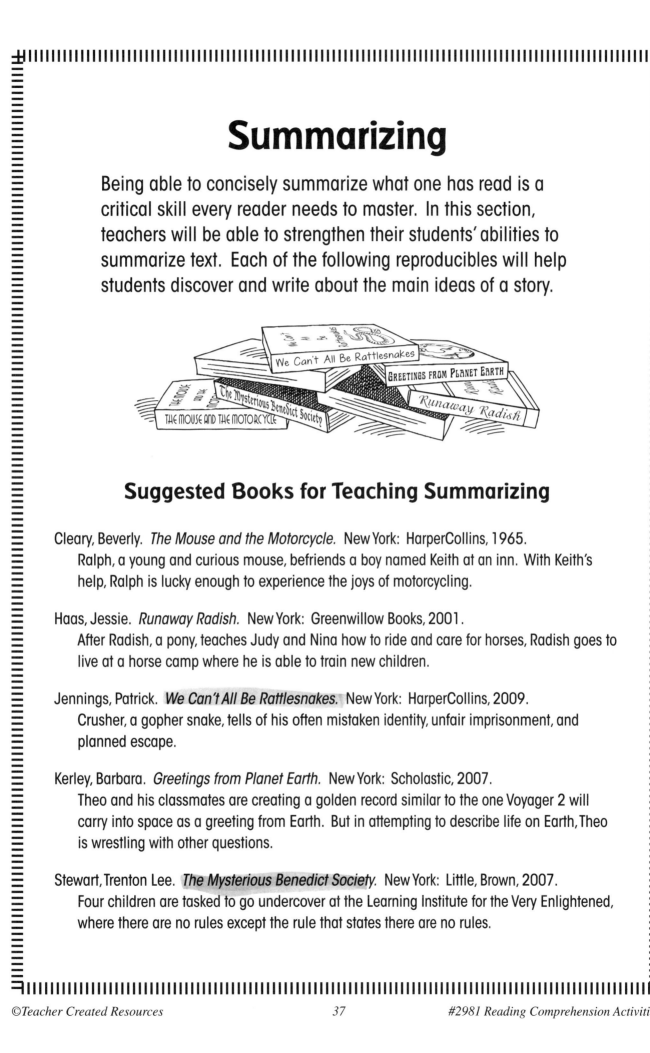

Suggested Books for Teaching Summarizing

Cleary, Beverly. *The Mouse and the Motorcycle.* New York: HarperCollins, 1965.
   Ralph, a young and curious mouse, befriends a boy named Keith at an inn. With Keith's help, Ralph is lucky enough to experience the joys of motorcycling.

Haas, Jessie. *Runaway Radish.* New York: Greenwillow Books, 2001.
   After Radish, a pony, teaches Judy and Nina how to ride and care for horses, Radish goes to live at a horse camp where he is able to train new children.

Jennings, Patrick. *We Can't All Be Rattlesnakes.* New York: HarperCollins, 2009.
   Crusher, a gopher snake, tells of his often mistaken identity, unfair imprisonment, and planned escape.

Kerley, Barbara. *Greetings from Planet Earth.* New York: Scholastic, 2007.
   Theo and his classmates are creating a golden record similar to the one Voyager 2 will carry into space as a greeting from Earth. But in attempting to describe life on Earth, Theo is wrestling with other questions.

Stewart, Trenton Lee. *The Mysterious Benedict Society.* New York: Little, Brown, 2007.
   Four children are tasked to go undercover at the Learning Institute for the Very Enlightened, where there are no rules except the rule that states there are no rules.

Activities for Summarizing

Soaring with Summaries

This enjoyable activity will allow students to summarize what they have read in a creative way. Copy Soaring with Summaries (page 39) for each student. Pass out six small pieces of yarn to each student. Have students read a book. In the boxes on the page, students will tell about the main character, setting, main problem, how the problem is solved, ending, and theme of the story. Students will cut out and hole-punch the boxes, joining them together with the yarn. For a visual decoration, hang their summaries from the ceiling.

Accordion Summaries

To begin this activity, copy Accordion Summaries (page 40) for each student. (Consider making multiple copies, back to back, for longer chapter books.) Have students fold the booklet on the lines into an accordion or "z" shape. This will give students three different sections for summarizing. Have students begin reading a book. For each chapter or section of the story read, students will write a summary and an analysis.

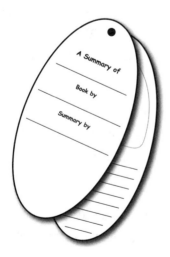

Question Summaries

To begin this activity, copy Question Summaries (pages 41–43) for each student. Pass out a brad or piece of yarn to each student. Have students read a book and then, using the ovals, describe the *who, what, where, when,* and *why* of their story. Have them draw pictures for each description, as well. Once they are finished, students will cut out and hole-punch the ovals. Afterwards, they will join together the ovals with the brad or piece of yarn.

Soaring with Summaries

Directions: Read a book, and then tell about each part of the story in the boxes below. Cut out and hole-punch the boxes, tying them together with yarn. Now your summary can soar!

My Summary of

Book by: _____

Summary by: _____

Describe the **main character** and **setting** of the story.

_____
_____
_____
_____
_____
_____
_____

Describe the **main problem** in the story.

_____
_____
_____
_____
_____

Tell how the problem was **solved**, and describe the **ending** of the story.

_____
_____
_____
_____
_____
_____
_____

The **theme** of this story is _____
_____
_____
_____

Accordion Summaries

Directions: Begin reading a book. Fold this page into an accordion or "z" shape. For each chapter or section of the story, write a summary and an analysis of what you have read.

Name: _____

Book Title: _____

Chapter or Pages: _____

Write a short summary of what you read.

_____
_____
_____
_____
_____

What thoughts did you have as you read?

_____
_____
_____
_____
_____

Chapter or Pages: _____

Write a short summary of what you read.

_____
_____
_____
_____
_____

What thoughts did you have as you read?

_____
_____
_____
_____
_____

Chapter or Pages: _____

Write a short summary of what you read.

_____
_____
_____
_____
_____

What thoughts did you have as you read?

_____
_____
_____
_____
_____

Question Summaries

Directions: Read a book. Using the ovals on this page and pages 42 and 43, describe the *who, what, where, when,* and *why* of the story. Draw pictures for each description, as well. Once you are finished, cut out the ovals and join them together using a brad or a piece of yarn.

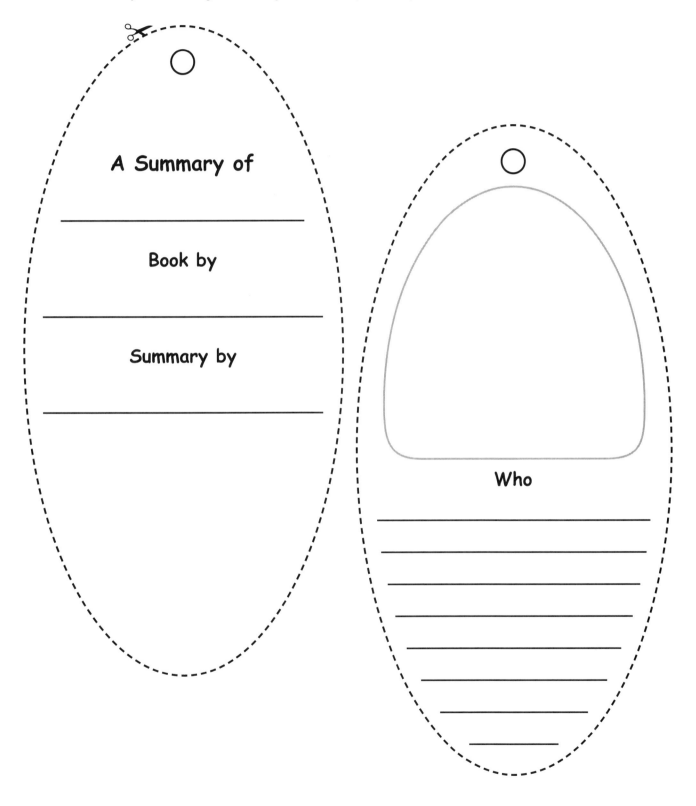

A Summary of

_____

Book by

_____

Summary by

_____

Who

_____
_____
_____
_____
_____
_____
_____
_____

Question Summaries *(cont.)*

Directions: Using the ovals on this page and pages 41 and 43, describe the *who, what, where, when,* and *why* of the story. Draw pictures for each description, as well. Once you are finished, cut out the ovals and join them together using a brad or a piece of yarn.

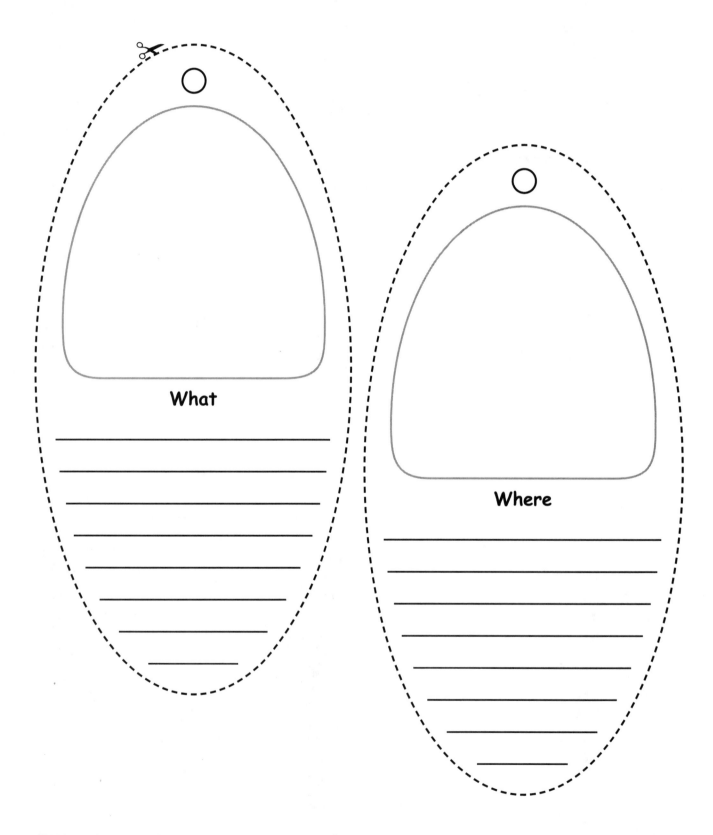

What

Where

Question Summaries *(cont.)*

Directions: Using the ovals on this page and pages 41 and 42, describe the *who, what, where, when,* and *why* of the story. Draw pictures for each description, as well. Once you are finished, cut out the ovals and join them together using a brad or a piece of yarn.

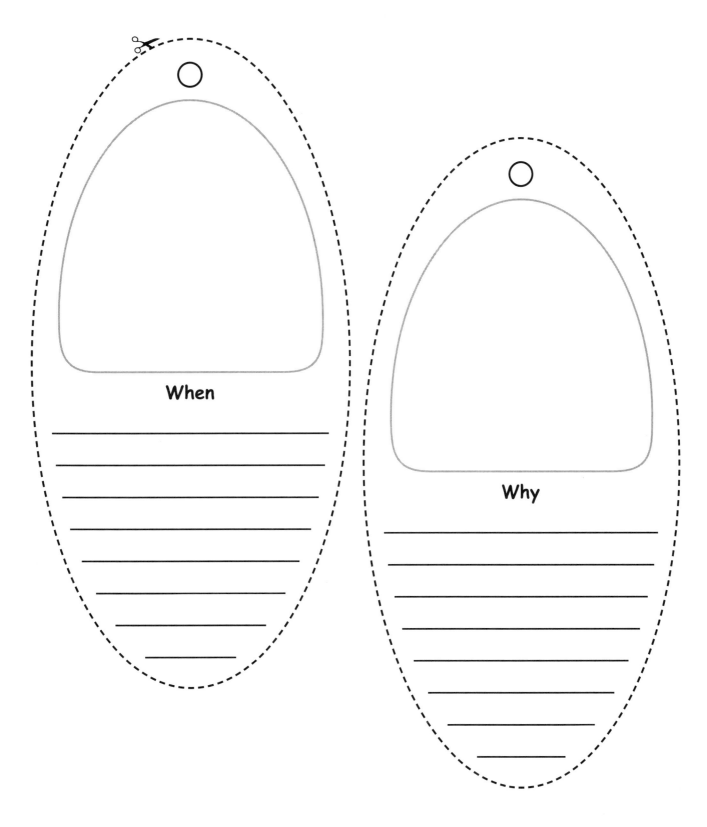

Sequencing

Understanding the order of a story is a skill that is essential for strong readers. In this section, students will be able to practice putting the events of a story in sequence from the beginning to the end. Fun activities and reproducibles will help students master story timelines.

Suggested Books for Teaching Sequencing

Norton, Mary. *The Borrowers.* New York: Harcourt, 1953.
    Miniature people live beneath the floorboards of an old country house. They "borrow" items from humans in order to outfit their own home—that is, until one of the borrowers is seen.

Rawls, Wilson. *Where the Red Fern Grows.* New York: Delacorte, 1961.
    Billy travels through the Ozarks with his coonhounds, during which time he embraces adventure and experiences a tragedy.

Ryan, Pam Munoz. *Paint the Wind.* New York: Scholastic, 2007.
    Maya has to move from California to Wyoming after her controlling grandmother has a stroke. At her new home, Maya feels a strong connection to horses. She also discovers a wild mare that her mother once rode.

Sachar, Louis. *Holes.* New York: Farrar, Straus and Giroux, 1998.
    The mantra at Camp Green Lake, a juvenile detention facility, is "If you take a bad boy and make him dig a hole every day in the hot sun, it will turn him into a good boy." Where there used to be a lake, there is now dry, flat land punctured by holes that have all been dug by troublesome boys—boys like Stanley Yelnats.

Selden, George. *The Cricket in Times Square.* New York: Farrar, Straus and Giroux, 1960.
    Lured by the smell of liverwurst, Chester Cricket hops into the picnic basket of some New Yorkers who are visiting the countryside. After Chester arrives in the big city, young Mario hears his chirp and wants to keep him as a pet. Chester is treated well, but he still misses his countryside home.

Activities for Sequencing

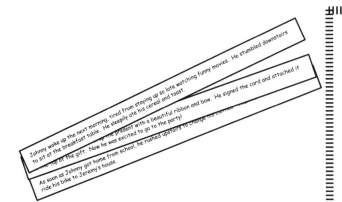

A Crazy Weekend

This activity will allow students to practice sequencing a story unknown to them. To begin, copy A Crazy Weekend (pages 46–47) for each student. Have students cut out the sentence strips on page 46 and place them in the correct order on page 47. Then have students glue each strip in the appropriate box.

Game Board Sequencing

This interactive activity will allow students to create their own board game while sequencing events from any text. Copy Game Board Sequencing (page 48), one per student. Then copy page 49, two per student. Give each student a piece of 12" x 18" construction paper. Then have students glue both copies of page 49 (the game board) onto the pieces of construction paper. Have students read a book and write the main events from their stories on the game board pieces. Each event from the story should have its own circle. Next, have students cut out the game board pieces. Then have students mix up their game board pieces and trade them with other students. Each student will read the new game board pieces and try to put them in the correct order. Once the pieces are in the correct order, the student will glue them onto the white spaces of the game board. The finished game boards can be displayed on a bulletin board titled "Game Board Sequencing."

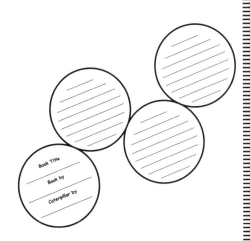

Sequencing Caterpillar

Copy Sequencing Caterpillar (pages 50–51) for each student. Make additional copies if needed for longer stories. Have students read a book. Then have students write the title and author in the first circle and describe the main events that happened in the text in the remaining circles. Once the events have been written out, students will cut out the circles, placing the events in order and glueing them onto pieces of 12" x 18" construction paper to create their own sequencing caterpillars. These can be decorated and displayed on a bulletin board.

A Crazy Weekend

Directions: Read the sentence strips below. Cut them out, and then glue them in the correct order on page 47.

Johnny woke up the next morning, tired from staying up so late watching funny movies. He stumbled downstairs to sit at the breakfast table. He sleepily ate his cereal and toast.

After dinner with Jeremy, Johnny rode his bike back home. He walked upstairs to get into his pajamas. He brushed his teeth and headed downstairs to the living room couch.

Johnny's mom helped him wrap the present with a beautiful ribbon and bow. He signed the card and attached it to the top of the gift. Now he was excited to go to the party!

Johnny was thrilled! It was Friday, and school was out. He was ready for his weekend to begin. Johnny had some great things planned.

Johnny and Jeremy played video games for three hours. Jeremy's mom bought a large pepperoni pizza that Jeremy and Johnny ate for dinner.

Johnny decided to watch some funny movies. He curled up on the couch with a blanket and watched funny movies until midnight. Then he went upstairs and crawled into bed.

As soon as Johnny got home from school, he rushed upstairs to change his clothes. Then he ran downstairs to ride his bike to Jeremy's house.

After eating his breakfast, Johnny slowly walked upstairs to get ready for the day. He got dressed and combed his hair. Then he walked downstairs to wrap a present for his cousin's birthday party, which was later on in the day.

A Crazy Weekend (cont.)

Directions: Read the sentence strips on page 46. Cut them out, and then glue them in the correct order below.

1	
2	
3	
4	
5	
6	
7	
8	

Game Board Sequencing

Directions: Read a book, and then tell about the main events from the story on the game board pieces below. *Note:* Each event from the story should have its own piece. Cut out the game board pieces and mix them up. Trade your pieces and game board with a classmate's, and try to put your classmate's pieces in the correct order. Then glue them onto the white spaces of the game board.

48

Game Board Sequencing (cont.)

Directions: After writing on, cutting out, and mixing up the game board pieces from page 48, glue both sheets of the game board (page 49) onto a piece of construction paper. Trade your pieces and game board with a classmate's, and try to put your classmate's pieces in the correct order. Then glue them onto the white spaces of the game board.

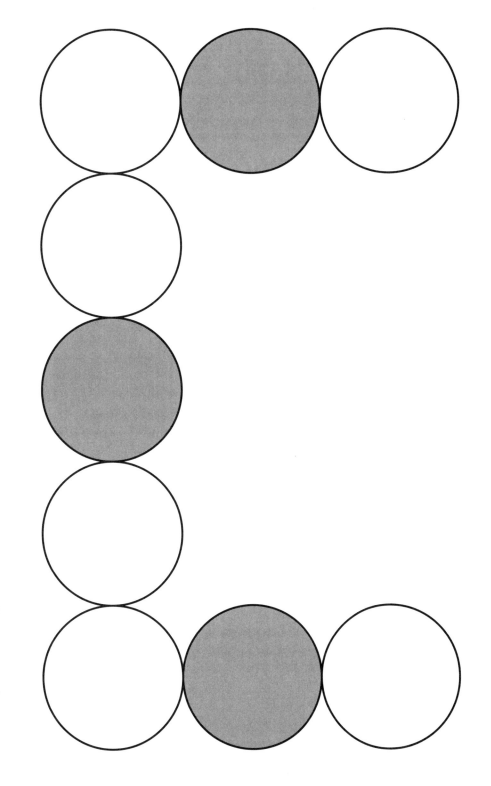

Sequencing Caterpillar

Directions: Read a book. Write the title and author in the first circle and use the remaining circles to describe the events that happened in the story. Cut out the circles. Put the events in order and glue them onto a piece of 12" x 18" construction paper to create your caterpillar.

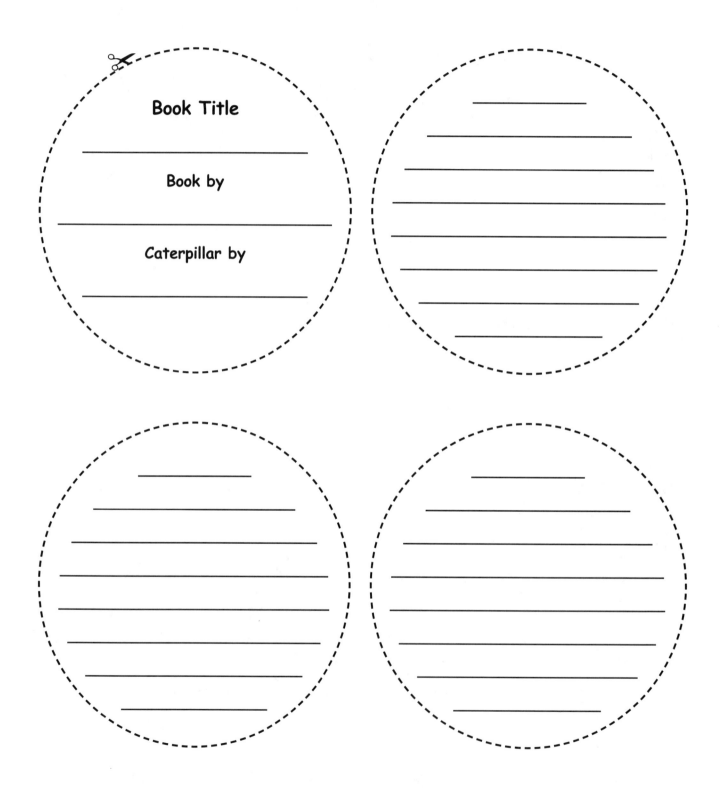

Book Title

_____

Book by

_____

Caterpillar by

_____

Sequencing Caterpillar *(cont.)*

Directions: Continue describing the events that happened in the story. Then cut out the circles. Put the events in order and glue them onto a piece of 12" x 18" construction paper to create your caterpillar.

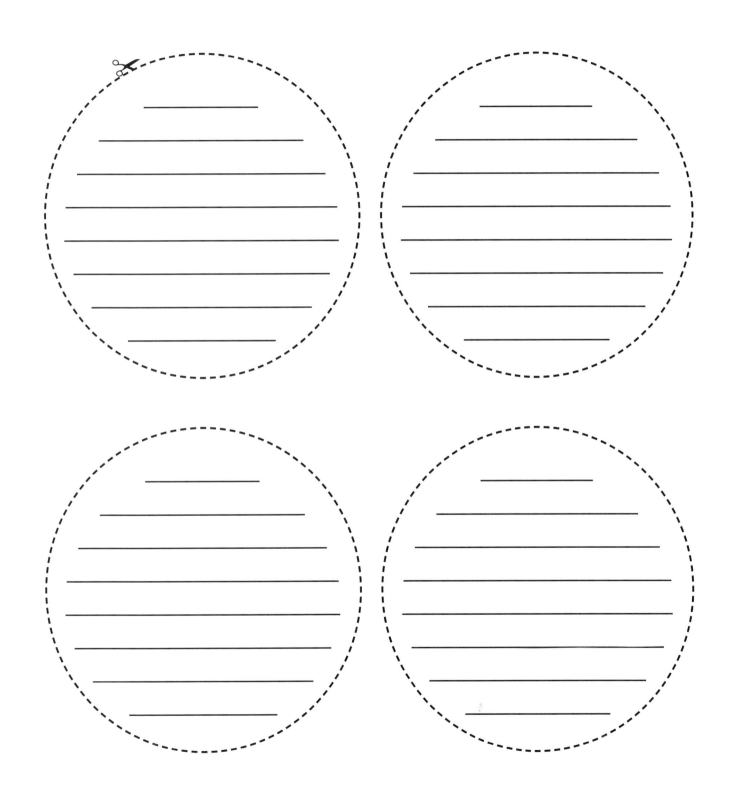

Retelling

As a component of sequencing, retelling a story with detail can be a difficult task. Nonetheless, retelling is a skill required of any keen reader. With these crafty activities and graphic organizers, teachers can help students identify the needed elements of a good retelling. With practice, students will be able to recall story details and write retellings using time-order words.

Suggested Books for Teaching Retelling

Atwater, Richard, and Florence Atwater. *Mr. Popper's Penguins.* Boston: Little, Brown, 1938.
 Mr. Popper, who is a house painter (in reality) and an Antarctic explorer (in his dreams), receives an unexpected delivery: a crate containing an Antarctic penguin.

Avi. *Poppy.* New York: Scholastic, 1995.
 Poppy, the mouse, wants to relocate her family as they have outgrown their current home. Mr. Ocax, the owl, who is in charge of where Poppy's family lives, denies the request. Poppy decides to move her family anyway, discovering some interesting information along the way.

Butterworth, Oliver. *The Enormous Egg.* New York: Little, Brown, 1956.
 Nate is surprised when he discovers that one of his family's hens has laid an enormous egg. He is determined to see it hatch.

Clements, Andrew. *Frindle.* New York: Simon & Schuster, 1996.
 When Nick Allen is assigned extra work by his vocabulary-loving teacher, he decides to have some fun with it. What results is a new word for pens ("frindle"!), after-school punishments, and national publicity.

Spinelli, Jerry. *Maniac Magee.* Boston: Little, Brown, 1990.
 Jeffrey Magee's talents seem too incredible to be true: he can run faster than anyone else, he can turn a "frog" ball into a home run, and he can untie knots that no one else can undo. Jeffrey, an orphan, is also blind to racism and wants nothing more than to find a safe home, regardless of where it is.

Activities for Retelling

Retelling, from Start to Finish

This activity will give students a step-by-step process for writing a complete retelling of any story. Copy Retelling, from Start to Finish (pages 54–55) for each student. Have students read a book and then give details for each part of the story in the boxes on page 54. Students will then use the information to write a detailed retelling of their story on page 55.

Chilly Retellings

This activity is a creative arts project that will allow students to retell any story. Copy Chilly Retellings (pages 56–57) for each student. For longer stories, make additional copies of page 57. Give each student two pieces of yarn. Have students read a book and then list the story information on the cloud. Next, have students retell their story on the snowflakes, writing each main event from the story on each snowflake. Lastly, have students cut out, hole-punch, and attach the snowflakes to the cloud using the yarn. *Note:* Students will need to make sure the snowflakes are in the correct order before attaching them to the clouds. For added fun, hang the chilly retellings from the ceiling.

Chart a Story

Copy Chart a Story (page 58), one per student. Have students read a book and then retell each part of the story using the graphic organizer.

Name _____ Date _____

Retelling, from Start to Finish

Directions: Read a book, and then complete the boxes below by giving details for each part of the story. Use this page to write a retelling of the story on page 55.

Book Title: _____

Who are the **characters**?	What is/are the **main setting(s)**?
_____	_____
_____	_____
_____	_____
_____	_____
_____	_____
_____	_____

How does the story **begin**?

_____

_____

_____

_____

What is the **main problem** in the story?

_____

_____

How is this problem **solved**?

_____

_____

_____

How does the story **end**?

_____

_____

_____

_____

Retelling, from Start to Finish *(cont.)*

Directions: Read a book, and then complete the boxes on page 54. Use your responses from page 54 to write a retelling of the story below.

_____
_____
_____
_____
_____
_____
_____
_____
_____
_____
_____
_____
_____
_____
_____
_____
_____
_____
_____
_____
_____
_____
_____

Chilly Retellings

Directions: Read a book, and then list the story information on the cloud below. Write the main events from the story on the snowflakes on page 57. Cut out and hole-punch the cloud and snowflakes. Attach them with yarn, making sure the events are in the correct order.

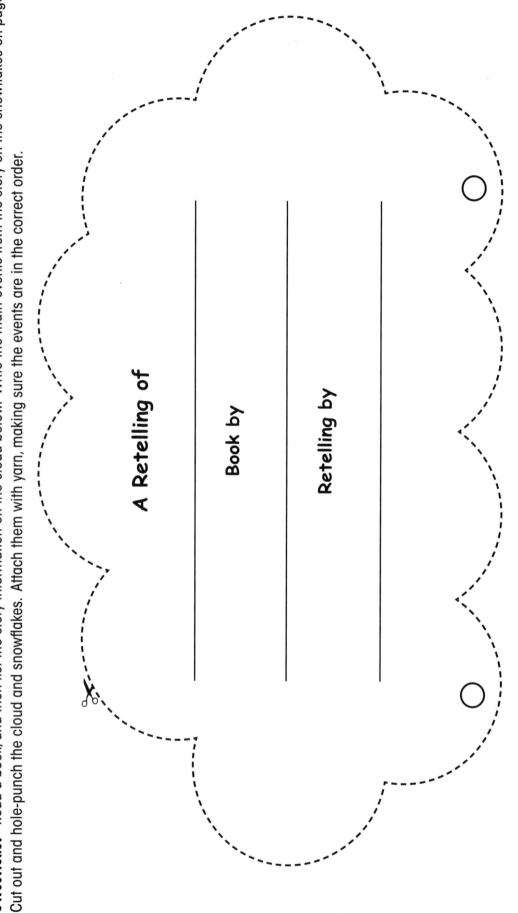

A Retelling of

Book by

Retelling by

Chilly Retellings *(cont.)*

Directions: Read a book, and then list the story information on the cloud on page 56. Write the main events from the story on the snowflakes below. Cut out and hole-punch the cloud and snowflakes. Attach them with yarn, making sure the events are in the correct order.

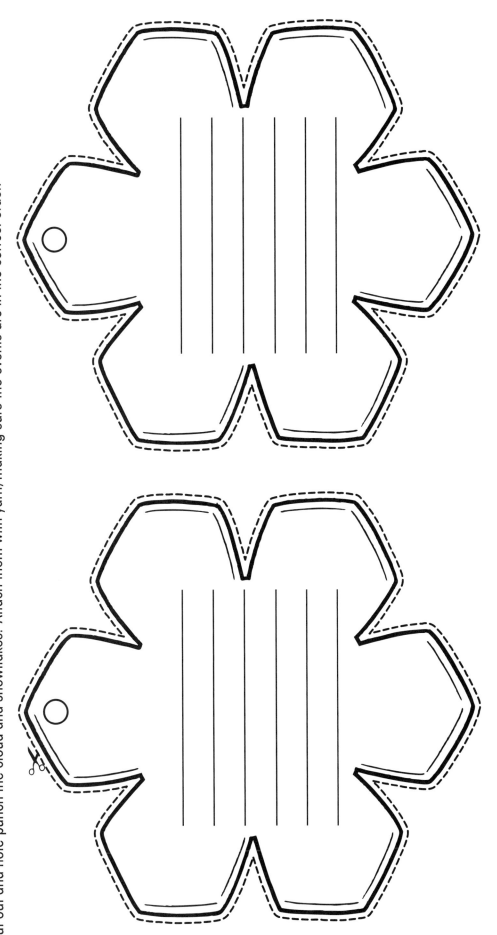

Chart a Story

Directions: Read a book, and then retell each part of the story below.

Book Title: _____

Book by: _____

Tell how the story begins, including the characters and setting.

_____
_____
_____
_____
_____
_____
_____
_____
_____

Explain in detail the main problem of the story.

_____
_____
_____
_____
_____
_____
_____
_____
_____

Tell how the problem is solved and how the story ends.

_____
_____
_____
_____
_____
_____
_____
_____
_____

Discovering the Main Idea

Discovering the main idea is a skill that is fundamental to basic reading comprehension. Using the activities and reproducibles in this section will help students find the main ideas and supporting details within any type of text.

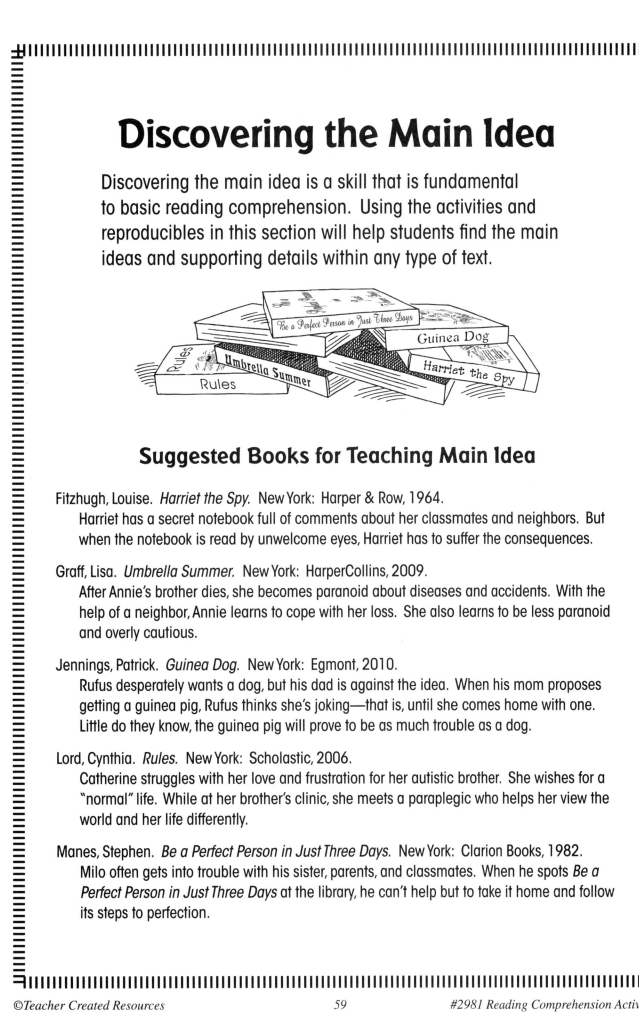

Suggested Books for Teaching Main Idea

Fitzhugh, Louise. *Harriet the Spy.* New York: Harper & Row, 1964.
    Harriet has a secret notebook full of comments about her classmates and neighbors. But when the notebook is read by unwelcome eyes, Harriet has to suffer the consequences.

Graff, Lisa. *Umbrella Summer.* New York: HarperCollins, 2009.
    After Annie's brother dies, she becomes paranoid about diseases and accidents. With the help of a neighbor, Annie learns to cope with her loss. She also learns to be less paranoid and overly cautious.

Jennings, Patrick. *Guinea Dog.* New York: Egmont, 2010.
    Rufus desperately wants a dog, but his dad is against the idea. When his mom proposes getting a guinea pig, Rufus thinks she's joking—that is, until she comes home with one. Little do they know, the guinea pig will prove to be as much trouble as a dog.

Lord, Cynthia. *Rules.* New York: Scholastic, 2006.
    Catherine struggles with her love and frustration for her autistic brother. She wishes for a "normal" life. While at her brother's clinic, she meets a paraplegic who helps her view the world and her life differently.

Manes, Stephen. *Be a Perfect Person in Just Three Days.* New York: Clarion Books, 1982.
    Milo often gets into trouble with his sister, parents, and classmates. When he spots *Be a Perfect Person in Just Three Days* at the library, he can't help but to take it home and follow its steps to perfection.

Activities for Discovering the Main Idea

Story Support

This activity will help students practice identifying supporting details for any main idea. Copy Story Support (page 61), one per student. Make additional copies if needed. Have students begin reading a chapter book. For each chapter, students will write the main idea and three supporting details.

Main Idea Flower

This activity will have students' ideas blooming! Copy Main Idea Flower (page 62), one per student. Give each student a narrow piece of green construction paper. Have students read a book and then write the main idea of the story in the circle. On the three petals, students will describe the setting, characters, and problem. On the leaf, students will write the conclusion of the story. Have students create a stem using the green construction paper. Next, have them write the book title on the stem. Then have them cut out and glue together the flower parts. These flowers can be displayed on a bulletin board titled "Main Idea Flowers."

Elephants eat all types of vegetation, including grass, vegetables, and fruit.

...phants can greet other elephants and make sound calls by using their trunks.

Elephants use their trunks to p... different items, such as leaves or ba...

...ult elephants can grow to be between 10 and 13 feet tall.

Elephant Sort

This activity will have students learning facts about the largest land mammal! Copy Elephant Sort (pages 63–64) for each student. Have students read and cut out the supporting details on page 63. Then have them read each main idea on page 64. Next, have students glue each supporting detail below the matching main idea.

Story Support

Directions: Begin reading a chapter book. For each chapter, write a main-idea sentence and three supporting details that describe the main idea.

Book Title: _____

Chapter: _____ Pages: _____	Chapter: _____ Pages: _____
Main Idea _____ _____ _____	**Main Idea** _____ _____ _____
Supporting Detail #1 _____ _____	**Supporting Detail #1** _____ _____
Supporting Detail #2 _____ _____	**Supporting Detail #2** _____ _____
Supporting Detail #3 _____ _____	**Supporting Detail #3** _____ _____

Main Idea Flower

Directions: Read a book, and then write the main idea of the story in the circle. On the three petals, describe the setting, characters, and problem from the story. On the leaf, write the conclusion of the story. Create a stem using green construction paper. Write the book title on the stem. Then cut out and glue all of the flower parts together.

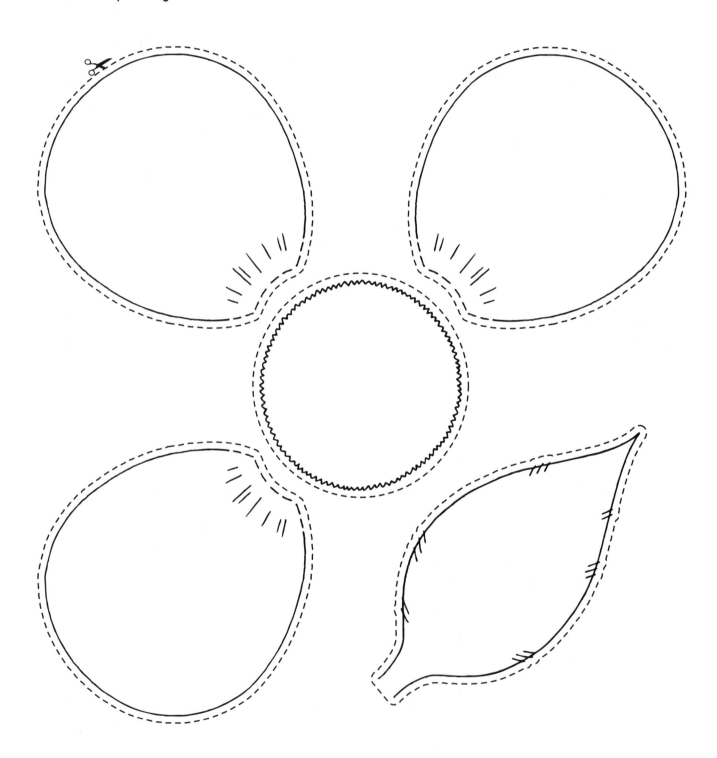

Elephant Sort

Directions: Read and cut out the supporting details below. Read each main idea on page 64. Glue each detail below the matching main idea.

They can devour almost as much as 300 pounds of vegetation a day.	Elephants use their trunks to pick up different items, such as leaves or bark.
Elephants can greet other elephants and make sound calls by using their trunks.	Elephants can weigh as much as seven tons.
Elephants take in water using their trunks and spray water on their backs to help cool themselves down.	They eat plants throughout the day, sometimes for up to 20 hours.
Adult elephants can grow to be between 10 and 13 feet tall.	To drink water, elephants use their trunks to suck up water and squirt it into their mouths.

Elephants eat all types of vegetation, including grass, vegetables, and fruit.

During hot days, elephants like to get into the mud.

African elephants are a little bit larger than Asian elephants.

By throwing some dust on their backs using their trunks, they protect their skin from the sun.

Elephant Sort

Directions: Read and cut out the supporting details below. Read each main idea on page 64. Glue each detail below the matching main idea.

They can devour almost as much as 300 pounds of vegetation a day.	Elephants use their trunks to pick up different items, such as leaves or bark.
Elephants can greet other elephants and make sound calls by using their trunks.	Elephants can weigh as much as seven tons.
Elephants take in water using their trunks and spray water on their backs to help cool themselves down.	They eat plants throughout the day, sometimes for up to 20 hours.
Adult elephants can grow to be between 10 and 13 feet tall.	To drink water, elephants use their trunks to suck up water and squirt it into their mouths.

Elephants eat all types of vegetation, including grass, vegetables, and fruit.

During hot days, elephants like to get into the mud.

African elephants are a little bit larger than Asian elephants.

By throwing some dust on their backs using their trunks, they protect their skin from the sun.

Elephant Sort (cont.)

Directions: Read each main idea. Read and cut out the supporting details on page 63. Glue each detail below the matching main idea.

Elephants use their trunks for many different things.		

African elephants are the largest living land mammal.		

Elephants are herbivores, or plant-eating animals.		

Spending days in the hot sun, elephants try to keep cool.		

Understanding Characterization

This section can help students grasp a necessary reading skill: identifying the character traits of main and supporting characters in the stories they read. These activities will give students different ways of looking at book characters. Whether describing their appearances or analyzing their personalities, students will soon understand characters from the inside out!

Suggested Books for Teaching Characterization

Blume, Judy. *Otherwise Known as Sheila the Great.* New York: Dutton, 1972.
Ten-year-old Sheila thinks she knows who she is: a funny, confident girl. However, after Sheila's friends have her face some of her fears, Sheila is second-guessing her opinion of herself.

Broach, Elise. *Masterpiece.* New York: Henry Holt, 2008.
Marvin is a beetle who, because of his artistic talent, can recreate Dürer works of art. Marvin, along with his 11-year-old friend, James, helps trap an art thief for the Metropolitan Museum of Art.

Hiaasen, Carl. *Flush.* New York: Alfred A. Knopf, 2005.
Noah and Abbey's dad is in jail for sinking a boat because, according to Dad, the owner of the boat was dumping sewage into local waters. Now it's up to Noah and Abbey to find evidence that will set their dad free.

Konigsburg, E. L. *From the Mixed-Up Files of Mrs. Basil E. Frankweiler.* New York: Atheneum, 1967.
Claudia and Jamie run away from home to the Metropolitan Museum of Art. While there, they become involved in an artistic mystery.

Porter, Eleanor. *Just David.* Boston: Houghton Mifflin, 1916.
David is a 10-year-old boy who has been raised by his father in the mountains. When David's father becomes ill, they have to leave their home for a more civilized area. But before they reach their destination, the father passes away. David is left to live with strangers in a foreign environment.

Activities for Understanding Characterization

Character Feelings

This activity will help students understand the various feelings a character may have in a story. Copy Character Feelings (page 67) for each student. Have students read each short passage and determine what feeling each character is expressing. Students will choose from the feelings in the Word Bank. After writing the feeling on the line, students will write down word clues from the text that support their answers. Students will learn to be observant while reading in order to recognize the feelings characters possess.

Character Trait Cards

Copy Character Trait Cards (pages 68–69) onto cardstock and laminate for durability. Cut out the cards. Copy Character Trait Cards Recording Sheet (page 70) for each student. Have students read the numbered passages and decide which traits the characters are showing. Once they match the passages to the traits, students will record their answers on the recording sheet. Students will then read the passage on page 70 and describe the main character using two words.

Character Collage

This activity will have students digging deeper into characters' personalities. Copy Character Collage (page 71), one per student. Make available a variety of materials, such as paint and colored tissue paper. Have students read a book and select one character from the story. Students will each decorate the figure on the page, using the various materials, according to what they think the characters look like. Then they will answer the questions about the characters.

Character Feelings

Directions: Read each passage. Each one illustrates a feeling that the character is expressing. Look at the feelings in the Word Bank. Choose the feeling that matches the passage and write it on the line. Include hints from the text that helped you decide on that feeling.

> **Word Bank**
>
> nervous   aggravated   apologetic   jubilant   nauseated

1. Dolly sits down at the table, her stomach grumbling. "I can't even take a bite; it hurts!" she says as she lays her head on the placemat.

   Dolly is feeling _____.

   Hints: _____

2. Sally's hands were shaking as she stood on the stage in front of a room full of people. Her legs felt weak, and she could not think of the first line of her speech.

   Sally was feeling _____.

   Hints: _____

3. Ted cannot contain himself! His team just won the championship! Along with some other fans, he is running around the baseball diamond yelling at the top of his lungs. His hands are waving high in the air.

   Ted is feeling _____.

   Hints: _____

4. Beth and Shelley were at the library last night preparing for their project. They had worked hard on the final project and couldn't wait to turn it in. Shelley left the library and told Beth she would take the project home and bring it to school the next day. As Beth got up to leave the library, she forgot the project. The next morning, when the girls were preparing for their presentation, Beth realized she did not have it. She looked at Shelley with tears in her eyes; Beth couldn't believe she had forgotten the project.

   Beth was feeling _____.

   Hints: _____

5. Ben and Henry were playing tetherball at recess. "I win!" said Ben. "No, I win!" yelled Henry. "Why do you always do that?" Ben yelled. "You never follow the rules. I am not playing with you anymore!" Ben continued.

   Ben was feeling _____.

   Hints: _____

Character Trait Cards

1 Jessica is sharing a bag of cookies with her little brother. She counts the cookies. There are a total of seven. She gives her brother three cookies and splits the last cookie in half to make sure everything is shared evenly.

Jessica is . . .

impatient

2 Leonard saw a small garden snake crawl into the bushes in his backyard. He put on some gloves and slowly walked toward the bushes. He was ready to catch the snake. His sister cried out, "Hurry, Leonard! I'm scared of snakes!"

Leonard was . . .

helpful

3 Patty and her mom want to make a cake for dessert. Patty goes to the pantry to get out the sugar, baking powder, and flour. Patty helps measure the ingredients. After everything is in the bowl, Patty mixes it all together for her mom.

Patty is . . .

gentle

4 Brady was very excited to taste the brownies his mother just put in the oven. Brady stared at the brownies as they baked. He looked at the timer, waiting for it to beep. Then he called out to his mom, "Are the brownies ready yet?"

Brady was . . .

fair

5 Taylor sees a little puppy wandering down the street. She slowly bends down and kindly pats the puppy on its back. She touches the back of its head with the lightest touch.

Taylor is . . .

brave

Character Trait Cards *(cont.)*

---

6 Marcus watched a new show on television about tigers. This made him wonder about all the different types of tigers. He decides to go to the library and check out some books about Bengal tigers and Siberian tigers. He wants to learn more!

Marcus is . . .

---

7 Jeremy asked his mother sweetly, "Can I please watch my favorite TV show?" After she agreed, he said, "Thank you!" After dinner that night, Jeremy said, "Thanks for a delicious dinner!" He then asked if he could be excused from the table.

Jeremy was . . .

---

8 Alexandra woke up with a frown on her face. She is not happy to be awake so early. She eats breakfast but complains, "My pancakes are too soggy!" Alexandra stomps out the door for school in an unhappy mood.

Alexandra is . . .

---

9 Donna got a new doll for her birthday. Her little sister, Kelly, asked if she could play with the doll, but Donna said, "No!" Kelly then asked if she could play with her toy blocks, and Donna said, "No!"

Donna was . . .

---

10 Mrs. Kline has a morning meeting at the office. She rushes out the door, grabbing some coffee on the way. After her meeting, she quickly eats her lunch. After work, she hurries out to pick up her kids from school.

Mrs. Kline is . . .

---

polite

busy

grouchy

curious

selfish

Character Trait Cards
Recording Sheet

Directions: Read each card and find the matching character trait. Write the character trait on the line next to the correct card number.

1. _____

2. _____

3. _____

4. _____

5. _____

6. _____

7. _____

8. _____

9. _____

10. _____

Directions: Read the passage below, and write two character traits that describe the character in the passage.

Jordan got off the phone with his neighbor, Mrs. Hipfield. He learned that she had just come home from the hospital. Jordan wanted to do something nice for Mrs. Hipfield, so he decided to make her a casserole for dinner. After finding everything he needed, Jordan put together the casserole and arranged some roses in a vase to bring to Mrs. Hipfield. He thought the smell of the roses would make her smile! Soon, the casserole finished baking, and Jordan took everything next door. Mrs. Hipfield was so thankful for Jordan's delicious dinner and the beautiful roses.

What two words would you use to describe Jordan?

_____   _____

Name _____ Date _____

Character Collage

Directions: Read a book and select one character from the story. Use different materials to decorate the face below so it looks like the character you chose. Then answer the questions about the character.

Book Title: _____

Who is this character? _____

What are three words that describe the personality of this character?

_____   _____   _____

How is this character feeling in the story? Why do you think so?

_____

_____

_____

What are some good qualities about this character?

_____

_____

_____

Describing the Setting

Beyond naming the place where a story happens, many students have trouble describing the setting, yet doing so is an invaluable skill for reading comprehension. The activities in this section will have students feeling as though they are interacting with the setting, as they focus on setting features, such as time, atmosphere, and seasons. Students will be able to use their senses to tell others about the wondrous places books can take them.

Suggested Books for Teaching Setting

Barrows, Annie. *The Magic Half.* New York: Bloomsbury, 2007.
   Miri is an overlooked child, but when her family moves into a new home, she feels lonelier than ever before. She soon spots a piece of glass in her room that, when looked through, reveals Molly, a girl from 1935. Now it is up to Miri to get Molly out.

Dahl, Roald. *Charlie and the Chocolate Factory.* New York: Knopf, 1964.
   In a contest initiated by Mr. Wonka himself, five lucky children get to explore the halls and walls of Willy Wonka's mysterious chocolate factory.

———. *James and the Giant Peach.* New York: Knopf, 1961.
   James, an orphan, is forced to live with his vile aunts after his parents pass away. After three years, he is absolutely miserable. When a magical crystal turns an ordinary-sized peach into one that is giant-sized, James is in luck! Now he can roll away in it and begin his own adventure.

Feldman, Jody. *The Gollywhopper Games.* New York: Greenwillow Books, 2008.
   Gil is training for the most important competition of his life: The Gollywhopper Games. If he wins, his family can move out of Orchard Heights—a place full of gossip and false friends.

Seidler, Tor. *Gully's Travels.* New York: Michael di Capua Books, 2008.
   Gulliver, a Lhasa Apso, enjoys his life of luxury—he has an owner that spoils him with fancy dog food and exotic trips overseas. But when the owner falls in love and needs to give Gulliver away, "Gully's" life of luxury comes to a screeching halt.

Activities for Describing the Setting

Setting It Up

This sorting activity will help students learn about the various ways a story's setting can be portrayed. Copy Setting It Up (page 74) for each student. Have students read each of the cards at the bottom of the page and determine which part of a setting the sentence is describing. Then have students cut out the cards and glue them in the correct category.

Sort Out the Setting

Copy Sort Out the Setting (pages 75–76) for each student. Have students read the setting cards on page 75. Next, have them determine if the cards describe a time, a place, or the atmosphere. Then have them write down the letter and sentence of each card on page 76.

Set the Scene

Copy Set the Scene (page 77) for each student. Have students read a book and then describe the main setting using details from the story, as well as their own senses. After answering the questions, students will draw detailed pictures depicting the settings from their story. This activity can be used as a quiz to see what students understand about setting using clues from their text.

Name _____ Date _____

Setting It Up

Directions: Read and cut out each card at the bottom of the page. Determine if the cards describe a time, place, or season. Glue the cards in the correct category.

Time	Place	Season

✂ -

The dazzling pumpkins were in full bloom, and there was a crisp chill in the air.	The enormous house was so colorful that it lit up the dark sky, and seeing the colors made me feel warm and cozy inside.	"Going outside will require gloves, a scarf, and a hat!" my mother yelled from the kitchen.
The sun was at its peak in the sky, and my stomach began to grumble.	We were finally there—I couldn't wait to feel the thrill of the rides and devour cotton candy.	It is the final day of class, and I can't wait to spend my free time swimming and hanging out with friends.
I have an extremely important appointment at 9:15 a.m., and I cannot be late.	The trees are decorated, and all the houses are so colorful and covered with lights. I love this time of year!	The stars were glowing brightly in the night sky. I gazed up, searching for a shooting star.
The sand felt amazing between my toes. I couldn't wait to construct a sand castle using the tools on the beach.	The alarm began to buzz. I couldn't believe it was time to get up.	The fresh air smelled wonderful, and it was amazing to see how big the trees were. I couldn't wait to set up my tent.

Sort Out the Setting

Directions: Read the setting cards below. Determine if the cards describe a time, a place, or the atmosphere. Then write down the letter and sentence of the card on page 76.

(A) The clouds covered the sun, casting shadows over the whole town.

(B) Jeffrey looked at his watch, which read 10:36 a.m.

(C) Everyone was excited for the fireworks to start at 8:00 p.m.!

(D) The snow-covered mountains looked as if they were topped with whipped cream.

(E) David found a comfortable booth in the corner of his favorite breakfast café.

(F) The rain clouds were gray and dreary, making me feel glum.

(G) Andy and his family drove to San Diego to go to the beach.

(H) Sophia knew it was time for bed after gazing for a while at the stars.

(I) The winds blew so hard that I was afraid a tornado was coming soon!

(J) I could hear the rustle of the leaves as the wind blew.

(K) After lunch, we took a long bike ride.

(L) The loud cheers from the crowd energized the tired players.

(M) As the sun rose, birds began to sing sweet songs.

(N) The coach watched as the team ran proudly onto the grassy football field.

(O) It was so quiet. I could almost hear a pin drop as I checked out some new books.

Name _____ Date _____

Sort Out the Setting *(cont.)*

Directions: Read the setting cards on page 75. Determine if the cards describe a time, a place, or the atmosphere. Then write down the letter and sentence of the card below.

Time

☐ _____

☐ _____

☐ _____

☐ _____

☐ _____

Place

☐ _____

☐ _____

☐ _____

☐ _____

☐ _____

Atmosphere

☐ _____

☐ _____

☐ _____

☐ _____

☐ _____

Set the Scene

Directions: Read a book, and then use details from the story, as well as your senses, to describe the main setting. Then draw a picture of the main setting.

Book Title: _____

Draw a picture of the main setting.

Where does the main setting of the story take place?

_____

_____

What can you hear in the setting?

_____

_____

_____

What is the atmosphere of the setting?

_____

_____

Finding the Problem and the Solution

This section focuses on a fundamental skill—finding the problem and the solution. The graphic organizers and comic strip craft can be reproduced and used many times with different texts. Students will be able to identify many problems and solutions using these various activities.

Suggested Books for Teaching Problem and Solution

Avi. *The Fighting Ground.* New York: HarperCollins, 1984.
At 13 years old, Jonathan is leaving to fight in the Revolutionary War. Little does he know, the real battle is within himself.

Cleary, Beverly. *Beezus and Ramona.* New York: HarperCollins, 1955.
Ramona is causing trouble, and her older sister, Beezus, is doing her best to stop her.

———. *Muggie Maggie.* New York: HarperCollins, 1990.
Maggie has decided to resist learning cursive. When asked how long it will take her to learn it, she says, "Maybe forever." Now she has to face the consequences of her defiant behavior.

Clements, Andrew. *Lunch Money.* New York: Simon & Schuster, 2005.
Greg, a sixth-grader, is hoping to make some extra money by selling comic books—that is, if his nemesis, Maura, doesn't get in his way.

Davies, Jacqueline. *The Lemonade War.* Boston: Houghton Mifflin, 2007.
Evan discovers that he and his younger sister, Jessie, will be in the same class for fourth grade. This leads to a lemonade-stand battle to see who can earn $100.00 first.

Activities for Finding the Problem and the Solution

What's the Problem?

Copy What's the Problem? (page 80), one per student. Have students read a book and then answer the questions about the main problem in the story. This activity can be used many times throughout the year with a variety of texts.

Problem and Solution Comic Strip

Copy Problem and Solution Comic Strip (pages 81–82) for each student. Make additional copies as needed. Have students begin reading a book, describing the problems and solutions as they develop in the story. Next, have students draw a picture for each problem and solution. Then have students cut out the comic strip pieces and glue them together in order. These comic strips can be displayed on a bulletin board titled "Problem and Solution Comic Strips."

Problem and Solution Storyboard

Copy Problem and Solution Storyboard (page 83), one per student. Using page 83 and a piece of 12" x 18" construction paper, students will create their own problem and solution storyboards. Students will begin by reading a book. Then they will write three problems and three solutions on the storyboard cards. Next, students will draw pictures for each problem and solution. After each storyboard card has been completed, students will cut out the cards and glue the problems and solutions in order onto the piece of construction paper. These storyboards can be decorated and displayed on a bulletin board titled "A Problem in Every Story."

What's the Problem?

Directions: Read a book, and then answer the questions about the main problem in the story.

Book Title: _____

What is the main problem in the story?

_____

_____

_____

_____

How does/do the character(s) feel about the problem? Why?

_____

_____

_____

Describe the steps it took to solve the problem.

_____

_____

_____

How does/do the character(s) feel once the problem is solved?

_____

_____

_____

Problem and Solution Comic Strip

Directions: Begin reading a book. Describe the problems and solutions as they develop in the story. Draw a picture for each problem and solution. Then cut out the comic strip pieces and attach them together in order.

My Comic Strip of

Book by

Comic Strip by

Problem: _____

Problem: _____

Solution: _____

Problem and Solution Comic Strip (cont.)

Directions: Continue describing the problems and solutions as they develop in the story. Draw a picture for each problem and solution. Then cut out the comic strip pieces and attach them together in order.

Problem: _____

Solution: _____

Solution: _____

The End

Problem and Solution Storyboard

Directions: Begin reading a book. Write three problems and three solutions from the story on the storyboard cards. Draw a picture for each problem and solution. Then cut out the cards and glue them in order onto a piece of construction paper.

Recognizing Cause and Effect

Teachers will be able to help explain cause and effect easily with the various activities in this section. The following pages include a matching activity and two graphic organizers. Using these activities, students will be able to practice identifying specific causes and effects within different stories.

Suggested Books for Teaching Cause and Effect

Catling, Patrick Skene. *The Chocolate Touch.* New York: HarperCollins, 1979.
   John Midas believes that chocolate is the best food in existence. But one day, after buying a special piece in a candy store, John's perspective on chocolate changes.

Reynolds Naylor, Phyllis. *Shiloh.* New York: Atheneum, 1991.
   When a young beagle runs away to Marty's house, he takes care of it. Marty is positive that the beagle has been abused, but Marty's parents force him to return the dog anyway. Marty feels he has no choice but to secretly rescue the dog.

Selznick, Brian. *The Invention of Hugo Cabret.* New York: Scholastic, 2007.
   The complex automaton that once belonged to Hugo's father now, due to his father's death, belongs to Hugo. Unfortunately, the automaton was damaged in a fire. Hugo's goal is to make the machine work again.

Sis, Peter. *The Wall: Growing Up Behind the Iron Curtain.* New York: Farrar, Straus and Giroux, 2007.
   In this autobiographical picture book, Peter tells how he grew up in Cold War-era Prague, during a time when children didn't ask questions. However, as time changed, people became more daring.

Van Allsburg, Chris. *Just a Dream.* Boston: Houghton Mifflin, 1990.
   Walter could care less about the environment—that is, until he has a dream that shows him a world abounding with trash and pollution. Upon waking up, he changes his habits.

Activities for Recognizing Cause and Effect

What Caused the Effect?

Copy What Caused the Effect? (page 86) for each student. Have students read a book and record three different causes and effects from the story. Then have students choose one of these sets to illustrate at the bottom of the page. To make their choice clear, students will write the number of their cause and effect (1, 2, or 3) in the box.

Cause and Effect Matchup Cards

Copy Cause and Effect Matchup Cards (page 87) onto cardstock and laminate for durability. Cut out the cards. Then copy Cause and Effect Matchup Cards Recording Sheet (page 88), one per student. Have students match each cause (letter cards) to its effect (number cards) and then record their answers on the recording sheet. For each number, they will write the letter and sentence that matches. For extra practice, challenge your students to create their own cause and effect matchup cards, and use the recording sheet again and again.

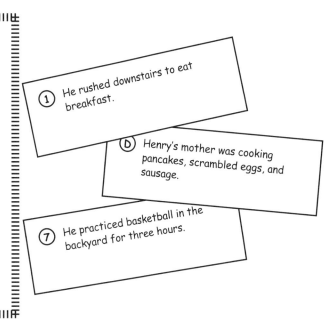

① He rushed downstairs to eat breakfast.

ⓑ Henry's mother was cooking pancakes, scrambled eggs, and sausage.

⑦ He practiced basketball in the backyard for three hours.

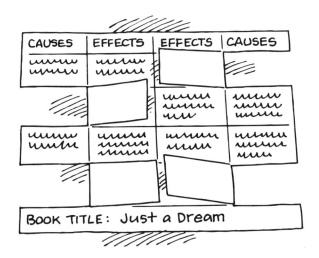

Cause and Effect Flap Booklet

Copy Cause and Effect Flap Booklet (page 89) for each student. Have students read a book and record the various causes and effects from the story. Then have students cut along the dotted lines and fold over the causes, hiding the effects. Now they have a Cause and Effect Flap Booklet!

What Caused the Effect?

Directions: Read a book, and then write about three different causes and effects from the story. Choose one of the causes and effects to illustrate at the bottom of the page. Write the number of your choice in the box.

Book Title: _____

① **Cause**

_____

_____

Effect

_____

_____

② **Cause**

_____

_____

Effect

_____

_____

③ **Cause**

_____

_____

Effect

_____

_____

○

Cause and Effect Matchup Cards

① He rushed downstairs to eat breakfast.

Ⓔ Henry had dirty socks and leftover food underneath his bed.

② His back was hurting when he got to his science class.

Ⓑ Today was class picture day at school.

③ Henry put on his best clothes and combed his hair to look handsome.

Ⓕ Henry's aunt from New York was arriving in town to spend a week.

④ Henry was saving his money to buy a dozen roses and a card.

Ⓓ Henry's mother was cooking pancakes, scrambled eggs, and sausage.

⑤ His room had a disgusting aroma.

Ⓒ Henry's favorite team made a great play.

⑥ He went with his mother to the airport.

Ⓐ Henry had a big tournament game to play next week.

⑦ He practiced basketball in the backyard for three hours.

Ⓗ His mother's birthday was on Saturday.

⑧ He shouted loudly at the television, "Great catch!"

Ⓖ Henry's backpack was filled with heavy books and supplies.

Cause and Effect Matchup Cards
Recording Sheet

Directions: Match each effect card (numbers) to the correct cause card (letters). Record your answers below. For each number, write the letter and sentence that matches.

1. ☐ _____

_____

2. ☐ _____

_____

3. ☐ _____

_____

4. ☐ _____

_____

5. ☐ _____

_____

6. ☐ _____

_____

7. ☐ _____

_____

8. ☐ _____

_____

Cause and Effect Flap Booklet

Directions: Read a book, and then write about different causes and effects from the story. Cut along the dotted lines and fold over the causes, hiding the effects. Now you have a Cause and Effect Flap Booklet!

Causes	Effects	Effects	Causes

Book Title: _____

Comparing and Contrasting

This reading skill helps students identify similarities and differences within a story or among different texts. Using the reproducible book activities, students will be able to find comparisons throughout the stories they are reading. An additional sorting activity will allow teachers to illustrate this concept using an unknown reading selection.

Suggested Books for Teaching Comparing and Contrasting

Ayres, Katherine. *Macaroni Boy.* New York: Delacorte, 2003.
   In Depression-era Pittsburgh, the Costa family owns a food warehouse. Mike Costa, a sixth-grader, thinks there is a connection between dead rats and his grandfather's worsening illness. He and his best friend investigate.

Frazee, Marla. *Couple of Boys Have the Best Week Ever.* Orlando, FL: Harcourt, 2008.
   Eamon and his friend, James, enroll in nature camp, spending their nights at Eamon's grandparents' house. The grandfather tries to bring out the "explorer" in the boys, but Eamon and James are more interested in having fun.

Paterson, Katherine. *The Great Gilly Hopkins.* New York: HarperCollins, 1978.
   Gilly, an 11-year-old foster child, dreams of reconnecting with her biological mother, who occasionally writes her letters. But her feelings change when her dream becomes a reality. Only then does she appreciate what she has: a foster family that genuinely loves her.

Peirce, Lincoln. *Big Nate: In a Class by Himself.* New York: HarperCollins, 2010.
   Nate, a sixth-grader, has a knack for getting detentions. But when he gets a fortune cookie that says he'll "surpass all others," he thinks luck will be on his side.

Rylant, Cynthia. *Gooseberry Park.* San Diego, CA: Harcourt, 1995.
   Three friends help save Stumpy and her babies after an ice storm destroys their home.

Activities for Comparing and Contrasting

Desert and Tundra Biomes

Students can learn as they go with this informational activity. Copy Desert and Tundra Biomes (pages 92–93) for each student. Have students read the Desert and Tundra Biomes passage (page 92). Then have them apply their knowledge of what they read to the graphic organizer activity (page 93). Have students cut out the facts about the biomes and glue them in the appropriate category.

Character Comparisons

Copy Character Comparisons (page 94) for each student. Have students read a book with at least two strong characters. Students will begin by writing the characters' names at the top of the page. On the heads, students will write about what the characters are thinking about in the story. Over the heart areas, students will write about how the characters are feeling in the story. On the bodies, students will write about what the characters are doing in the story. Then, in the middle of the page, students will list the ways that the two characters are alike.

Alike and Different

Copy Alike and Different (page 95), one per student. Have students read a book with at least two strong characters. Then have students compare and contrast the characters using details from the story.

Desert and Tundra Biomes

There are many different biomes in the world. Two biomes that have many similarities are the desert biome and the tundra biome. Each of these biomes covers one-fifth of the world's surface. Although these places are similar in many ways, they each have some unique features that set them apart.

Deserts are very hot, dry places. They receive less than ten inches of rainfall each year. With very little water in the desert, special animals and plants found in these areas can adapt to living in this type of environment. One of the main types of plant life found in the desert is the cactus. Temperatures in the desert can be very hot during the day; however, at night it can become cold. There are many deserts in the world—the largest, the Sahara Desert, is located in Africa.

The tundra regions are also considered to be very dry and cold. They receive very little rainfall—less than ten inches each year. The tundra regions are treeless places where there is permafrost,

a permanently frozen layer of soil. In this biome, there are few animals and plants that can handle the rough setting. Some of the animals that have adapted to the tundra regions are polar bears, arctic foxes, and grey wolves. The tundra can be found in few places around the world, such as near the Arctic Ocean.

Both these biomes are very unique and the most difficult to survive in on Earth.

Desert and Tundra Biomes *(cont.)*

Directions: Read the Desert and Tundra Biomes passage on page 92. Then use the passage to help you with the activity below. Cut out the facts about the different biomes and glue them in the correct category.

Tundra	Both	Desert

This biome covers about one-fifth of Earth's surface.

A common animal found in this biome is the grey wolf.

This biome can be extremely hot during the day and chilly at night.

This biome can be found in the Arctic region in the North.

This biome has permafrost, a frozen layer of soil.

Animals in this biome can adapt to the severe conditions.

This biome receives less than ten inches of rain every year.

This biome's most common plant is the cactus.

The largest type of this biome can be found in Africa.

Character Comparisons

Directions: Read a book, and then select two strong characters from the story. Write their names on the lines. Describe each character on the figures. Then list how the characters are alike in the center box.

Book Title: _____

1st Character's Name: _____

2nd Character's Name: _____

The character is thinking . . .

The character is feeling . . .

The character is doing . . .

Ways the characters are alike:

The character is thinking . . .

The character is feeling . . .

The character is doing . . .

Name _____   Date _____

Alike and Different

Directions: Read a book, and then select two strong characters from the story. Write their names on the lines. Tell how they are alike and different using details from the story.

Book Title: _____

1st Character's Name: _____   2nd Character's Name: _____

Alike	Different
What personality traits do these characters have in common?	How do these characters differ in their personalities?
What feelings do these characters have in common?	What feelings do these characters have that differ from each other?
In what other ways are these characters alike?	In what other ways are these characters different?

         #2981 Reading Comprehension Activities

Answer Key

Pages 15–16

1. disgusting	6. pretty
2. tired	7. save
3. sad	8. excited
4. thankful	1. polite
5. scared	2. shy

Page 20

1. This passage is about a family. Hints: Answers will vary but may include "my family," "we," "my brother," "my sister," etc.

2. The family is going on vacation. Hints: Answers will vary but may include "packing our suitcases," "go to the airport," "getting to the hotel," "sightseeing," etc.

3. Answers will vary but may include waterfall, Niagara Falls, etc. Hints: "water was like hearing thunder," "cool mist," "wall of water," "cascaded down," etc.

4. Answers will vary.

Pages 21–23

1. taking out the trash
2. doing his homework
3. washing some dishes
4. wrapping a present
5. taking a hike
6. watching a football game
7. watching a movie
8. fishing

Kevin is snowboarding.

Pages 46–47

1. Johnny was thrilled! It was Friday, and school was out. He was ready for his weekend to begin. Johnny had some great things planned.

2. As soon as Johnny got home from school, he rushed upstairs to change his clothes. Then he ran downstairs to ride his bike to Jeremy's house.

3. Johnny and Jeremy played video games for three hours. Jeremy's mom bought a large pepperoni pizza that Jeremy and Johnny ate for dinner.

4. After dinner with Jeremy, Johnny rode his bike back home. He walked upstairs to get into his pajamas. He brushed his teeth and headed downstairs to the living room couch.

5. Johnny decided to watch some funny movies. He curled up on the couch with a blanket and watched funny movies until midnight. Then he went upstairs and crawled into bed.

6. Johnny woke up the next morning, tired from staying up so late watching funny movies. He stumbled downstairs to sit at the breakfast table. He sleepily ate his cereal and toast.

7. After eating his breakfast, Johnny slowly walked upstairs to get ready for the day. He got dressed and combed his hair. Then he walked downstairs to wrap a present for his cousin's birthday party, which was later on in the day.

8. Johnny's mom helped him wrap the present with a beautiful ribbon and bow. He signed the card and attached it to the top of the gift. Now he was excited to go to the party!

Pages 63–64

African Elephants are the largest living land mammal.

- Elephants can weigh as much as seven tons.
- African elephants are a little bit larger than Asian elephants.
- Adult elephants can grow to be between 10 and 13 feet tall.

Elephants use their trunks for many different things.

- Elephants use their trunks to pick up different items, such as leaves or bark.
- Elephants can greet other elephants and make sound calls by using their trunks.
- To drink water, elephants use their trunks to suck up water and squirt it into their mouths.

Spending days in the hot sun, elephants try to keep cool.

- During hot days, elephants like to get into the mud.
- Elephants take in water using their trunks and spray water on their backs to help cool themselves down.
- By throwing some dust on their backs using their trunks, they protect their skin from the sun.

Elephants are herbivores, or plant-eating animals.

- Elephants eat all types of vegetation, including grass, vegetables, and fruit.
- They can devour almost as much as 300 pounds of vegetation a day.
- They eat plants throughout the day, sometimes for up to 20 hours.

Page 67

1. nauseated; hints: "stomach grumbling," "it hurts," "lays her head on the placemat"

2. nervous; hints: "hands were shaking," "legs felt weak," "could not think of the first line"

3. jubilant; hints: "cannot contain himself," "won the championship," "is running around," "yelling," "hands are waving"

4. apologetic; hints: "tears in her eyes," "couldn't believe she had forgotten"

5. aggravated; hints: "Ben yelled," "You never follow the rules," "I am not playing with you anymore!"

Pages 68–70

1. fair	7. polite
2. brave	8. grouchy
3. helpful	9. selfish
4. impatient	10. busy
5. gentle	Answers will vary.
6. curious	

Page 74

Time

- I have an extremely important appointment at 9:15 a.m., and I cannot be late.
- The sun was at its peak in the sky, and my stomach began to grumble.
- The alarm began to buzz. I couldn't believe it was time to get up.
- The stars were glowing brightly in the night sky. I gazed up, searching for a shooting star.

Place

- The sand felt amazing between my toes. I couldn't wait to construct a sand castle using the tools on the beach.
- We were finally there—I couldn't wait to feel the thrill of the rides and devour cotton candy.
- The fresh air smelled wonderful, and it was amazing to see how big the trees were. I couldn't wait to set up my tent.
- The enormous house was so colorful that it lit up the dark sky, and seeing the colors made me feel warm and cozy inside.

Season

- The dazzling pumpkins were in full bloom, and there was a crisp chill in the air.
- It is the final day of class, and I can't wait to spend my free time swimming and hanging out with friends.
- The trees are decorated, and all the houses are so colorful and covered with lights. I love this time of year!
- "Going outside will require gloves, a scarf, and a hat!" my mother yelled from the kitchen.

Pages 75–76

Time

B, C, H, K, M

Place

D, E, G, N, O

Atmosphere

A, F, I, J, L

Pages 87–88

1. D	5. E
2. G	6. F
3. B	7. A
4. H	8. C

Pages 92–93

Tundra

- This biome can be found in the Arctic region in the North.
- This biome has permafrost, a frozen layer of soil.
- A common animal found in this biome is the grey wolf.

Both

- This biome covers about one-fifth of Earth's surface.
- Animals in this biome can adapt to the severe conditions.
- This biome receives less than ten inches of rain every year.

Desert

- This biome can be extremely hot during the day and chilly at night.
- This biome's most common plant is the cactus.
- The largest type of this biome can be found in Africa.